Michael S. Woods, M.D., M.M.M.

Foreword by Marshall Goldsmith, Ph.D.

S0-AIJ-262

Civil Leadership

The Final Step to Achieving Safety, Quality, Innovation, and Profitability in Health Care

Joint Commission Resources

Manager, Publications: Paul Reis
Project Manager: Andrew Bernotas
Associate Director, Production: Johanna Harris
Executive Director: Catherine Chopp Hinckley, Ph.D.
Joint Commission/JCR Reviewers: Paul Schyve, M.D., Catherine Chopp Hinckley, Ph.D.
Other Reviewer: Darrell Ranum, J.D., C.P.H.R.M.

Joint Commission Resources Mission
The mission of Joint Commission Resources (JCR) is to continuously improve the safety and quality of health care in the United States and in the international community through the provision of education, publications, consultation, and evaluation services.

Joint Commission Resources educational programs and publications support, but are separate from, the accreditation activities of The Joint Commission. Attendees at Joint Commission Resources educational programs and purchasers of Joint Commission Resources publications receive no special consideration or treatment in, or confidential information about, the accreditation process.

The inclusion of an organization name, product, or service in a Joint Commission Resources publication should not be construed as an endorsement of such organization, product, or service, nor is failure to include an organization name, product, or service to be construed as disapproval.

This publication is designed to provide accurate and authoritative information in regard to the subject matter covered. Every attempt has been made to ensure accuracy at the time of publication; however, please note that laws, regulations, and standards are subject to change. Please also note that some of the examples in this publication are specific to the laws and regulations of the locality of the facility. The information and examples in this publication are provided with the understanding that the publisher is not engaged in providing medical, legal, or other professional advice. If any such assistance is desired, the services of a competent professional person should be sought.

Joint Commission Resources, Inc. (JCR), a not-for-profit affiliate of The Joint Commission, has been designated by The Joint Commission to publish publications and multimedia products. JCR reproduces and distributes these materials under license from The Joint Commission.

Printed in the U.S.A. 5 4 3 2 1

Requests for permission to make copies of any part of this work should be mailed to
Permissions Editor
Department of Publications
Joint Commission Resources
One Renaissance Boulevard
Oakbrook Terrace, Illinois 60181 U.S.A.
permissions@jcrinc.com

ISBN: 978-1-59940-405-9
Library of Congress Control Number: 2010921642

For more information about Joint Commission Resources, please visit http://www.jcrinc.com.

To my children, first and always in my heart and mind forever.

Contents

Foreword

by Marshall Goldsmith, Ph.D.

The concept and practice of civil leadership is here expanded upon by Michael S. Woods, M.D., M.M.M., in an obvious, yet all too often neglected aspect of what it is to lead. It would seem that everyone—health care professionals included—would know that civility in leadership would grease the wheels of success. However, daily I am in contact with leaders around the world, and civility in leadership is an issue that I see brought to the surface time and again. The damages of incivility can be huge, and can not only halt personal progress of the leader and those being led, but can halt organizational progress—and be a great barrier to success of leaders, their people, and their teams.

This great book, *Civil Leadership: The Final Step to Achieving Safety, Quality, Innovation, and Profitability in Health Care,* is built on, among other things, the foundations of Peter Drucker's four basic competencies of leadership, Warren Bennis's four lessons of self-knowledge, and Chris Argyris's four core values of individuals. These fundamental concepts lead me to ponder a central dimension of the effective leader as foretold by Drucker several years ago: "Leaders of the past knew how to tell. Leaders of the future must know how to ask." A significant attribute of civil leadership is "to ask" others for feedback in order to gain self-knowledge.

Self-knowledge can be very helpful in relationships, both at work and at home. It can mean the difference between getting ahead, staying the same, or even falling back and behind. Recently I wrote a book with 21 annoying habits that leaders around the world have developed. Such bad habits are very simple to identify, but they are hard for leaders to spot or admit to themselves, and thus these habits are easily capable of hindering leaders' progress greatly. For instance, speaking when angry, not listening, and withholding information are just a few annoying interpersonal issues that leaders have.

Leaders who are willing to ask those with whom they work for feedback about themselves are willing to listen to the response, and will work on getting better in the areas highlighted, are the same leaders who achieve the greatest success for their organizations and themselves. It's a simple formula for leadership: ask, listen, and act. Even more important as the destructive habits disappear—it can be a simple formula for civility in leadership, a critical subject in today's changing workplace and the subject of this wonderful book.

Marshall Goldsmith, Ph.D. is a leadership expert and author of *New York Times* best sellers *MOJO: How to Get It, How to Keep It, and How to Get It Back When You Lose It!* (2010) and *What Got You Here Won't Get You There* (2007).

Introduction

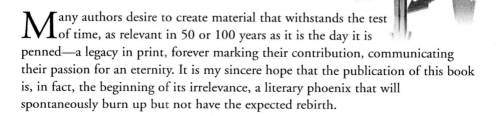

M any authors desire to create material that withstands the test of time, as relevant in 50 or 100 years as it is the day it is penned—a legacy in print, forever marking their contribution, communicating their passion for an eternity. It is my sincere hope that the publication of this book is, in fact, the beginning of its irrelevance, a literary phoenix that will spontaneously burn up but not have the expected rebirth.

The reader may find this odd, but if this book were to be successful in creating a gut-level, inflamed desire within the health care industry to achieve—in fact, demand—civility and a commitment to relationship-based principles and communication, and the pervasive, visible practice of the concepts—actually *living* the principles—it would make reprinting or future editions of this book unnecessary. I would gladly give up any associated legacy if such an outcome could be achieved. If this were accomplished, the health care industry, one sixth of the entire U.S. economy, would witness unparalleled improvement in quality, safety, and profitability.

I seriously doubt such transformational change will happen. Changing anything that is so big that it accounts for nearly 17% of the gross domestic product, the largest segment of the U.S. economy,[1] can't be done very fast. Clearly, health care is a major driver in the monetary world. But I would argue that the suppliers of health care—providers—unlike suppliers in virtually any other industry, have not responded to patently obvious market forces. There is an ever-expanding demand for health care services, yet we have a consistently declining critical resource to deliver and meet need: providers. Pair this undeniable reality with declining provider reimbursement and increasing overhead and regulatory pressures by state and federal agencies, and the outcome is almost certainly total industry failure—at least without significant, radical, sustained changes in the structure of the system and industrywide innovation.

Saying health care is complex is a laughable remark; it is beyond complex, affecting every citizen and every institution or business. Regardless of the topic—the economics of health care, the payers, providers and their training systems, the myriad state and federal governmental agencies, lawyers, hospitals, pharmaceutical companies, insurers—no one is immune to justified, well-deserved criticism. This complexity paradoxically, and somewhat disturbingly, inoculates each of the above-noted participants from sole responsibility of having created the complex morass that is rightly maligned by just about anyone who knows anything about health care and *everyone* who has had the need to access the industry as a client—that is, patients.

Yes, the number and magnitude of issues the industry faces are daunting. Those issues have and will continue to be examined and discussed for many years to come. But this book's focus is on the ways we, as providers—the ones closest to the action—can affect change *directly.*

Leadership from providers must drive the needed change, and it must be guided by very straightforward concepts such as civility, with an accurate perspective of the complexity of the challenge. One important factor is our behavior. Importantly, the first step we must take is to be *willing* to commit to the kind of change we as providers would like to see. Creating change, however, isn't enough. We need to *sustain* the effort and fix the outcome firmly into place by walking the talk—through personal demonstration to young providers, those in training. We need to teach them that acting with civility is not just important to getting along with our coworkers and patients, but it is *critical* to creating and optimizing the quality and safety initiatives that everyone in the industry desires. In fact, we can never achieve the kind of quality and safety we should have without such commitment to civility. They need to understand that there is an economic benefit to civility that is unavailable to those who do not live its principles—better employee and customer retention, higher patient satisfaction, and lower liability.

The respect we will regain as providers by focusing on the right things—relationship driving civil leadership, for one—will enable us to reclaim the profession. The credibility we will build through those relationships, from patients to the C-suite players, will allow us to have a more direct effect on what is happening and to promote the kinds of radical innovation needed to save the industry. We will no longer be sitting by idly, being acted upon. Rather, we will be the instruments of change in health care. Thomas Paine perhaps said it best in his manifesto, *Common Sense:*

> *Perhaps the sentiments contained in the following pages are not yet sufficiently fashionable to procure them general favor; a long habit of not thinking a thing wrong, gives it a superficial appearance of being right, and raises at first a formidable outcry in defense of custom. But the tumult soon subsides. Time makes more converts than reason.*[2(p. 5)]

References

1. Park A.: America's health checkup. *Time pp. 41–68,* Dec. 1, 2008.
2. Paine T.: *Common Sense.* In Foner E. (ed.): *Thomas Paine: Collected Writings.* New York: Library of America, 1995, pp. 5–59.

Chapter One
Relationship-Based Civil Leadership

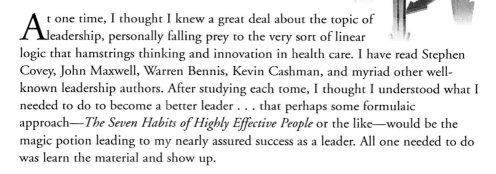

At one time, I thought I knew a great deal about the topic of leadership, personally falling prey to the very sort of linear logic that hamstrings thinking and innovation in health care. I have read Stephen Covey, John Maxwell, Warren Bennis, Kevin Cashman, and myriad other well-known leadership authors. After studying each tome, I thought I understood what I needed to do to become a better leader . . . that perhaps some formulaic approach—*The Seven Habits of Highly Effective People* or the like—would be the magic potion leading to my nearly assured success as a leader. All one needed to do was learn the material and show up.

Many of us in health care have an inherent discomfort with concepts that do not have nice, neat, nailed-down definitions. After all, great comfort comes to those of us who regularly feed at the trough of linear, logical thinking when rigid definition—even if only partially accurate—can be assigned to nebulous concepts. Witness the recent attempts by the Accreditation Council for Graduate Medical Education (ACGME) and The Joint Commission to instill the six competencies into medical practice (*see* Box 1-1, page 2). At least three of the competencies defy neat definitions: *professionalism, communication skills,* and *interpersonal skills. Leadership,* as I have come to learn, also defies definition. This is highlighted by the fact that one often sees definitions of *professionalism,* for example, that describe it in terms of recognized anti-traits, such as yelling, berating, belligerence, arrogance, harassment. . . .

ACGME is requiring residency training programs to document that their graduates are competent in these items, and the Joint Commission has adopted the same expectations for hospitals in its "Medical Staff" chapter of the comprehensive accreditation manual.

When one tries to place definitions around nebulous concepts—concepts such as strategy, leadership, communication, interpersonal skills, and professionalism—to "academize" the terms and tame them, mold them into understandable bite-size

Box 1-1. The Six Competencies, as Defined by the Accreditation Council for Graduate Medical Education and The Joint Commission

1. Patient care
2. Medical/clinical knowledge
3. Practice-based learning and improvement
4. Interpersonal communication skills
5. Professionalism
6. Systems-based practice

pieces that are so auto-digested that we don't even need to chew, a strange but reproducible phenomenon occurs: The very process of definition results in the concepts losing "their emotional resonance, no longer expressing the reality that practitioners originally tried to capture."[1(p. 17)] In trying to define each of these concepts, and perhaps particularly leadership, in the attempt to "dissect a living phenomenon, the skeleton may be revealed while the specimen dies."[1(p. 17)]

It has become increasingly apparent to me that the type of leadership needed from situation to situation is never the same, and, therefore, leadership is resistant to generic definitions and formulas. The same can be said, by the way, regarding communication, interpersonal skills, and professionalism. These concepts are made up of a collection of behaviors that manifest differently at different times, tailored to the specific situation, with a broad range of individual competence, creating an unreproducible whole. To illustrate, take the concept of integrity—the "sense of being truly genuine—which proves crucial to visionary leadership, and makes it impossible to translate into a general formula."[1(p. 21)] There will never be another Dwight D. Eisenhower because the situations he confronted will never be the same. We can study how he was and what he did, and we can codify his skill set, but we will never be able to convert his leadership into a reproducible formula for broad, generic application.

While acknowledging that there will never be another Eisenhower, it is worth noting that the great general and president wrote his son John, at the time a West Point cadet, "The one quality that can be developed by studious reflections and practice is the leadership of men."[2(p. 214)] I believe what Eisenhower was communicating to John was that the *skills* needed to lead effectively *can be learned.* How an individual applies those lessons, however, and whether he or she is effective in applying the learnings will differ based upon the situation *and* the individual. In other words, leadership and the application of the aggregate of those things that make up effective leadership is *situational,* assuming that the individual has acquired a set of baseline skills.

Peter Drucker, the late management guru, widely considered the greatest thinker on this topic of the twentieth century, thought that individuals can lead through virtually any set of circumstances and challenges, using four basic competencies (*see* Table 1-1, page 4).[3] For each of the competencies Drucker described, I have used a single word (in bold) to assist the reader in remembering the concept.

Drucker felt quite strongly that "pettiness and ego [are] the enemy of effective leadership."[3(p. 202)] Health care providers are often justifiably accused of both of these transgressions, and unfortunately, those accusations are often driven by financial or protectionist turf battles, thinly veiled as concerns for patient quality or safety.

The Importance of Self-Knowledge

Drucker's four simple competencies—*listening, clarity, accountability,* and *stewardship*—are critical to all individuals in leadership roles. Self-monitoring of one's behaviors is important in the development of such skills. In other words, leaders become increasingly effective by having a very deep understanding of *themselves.* Leadership isn't about being perfect but creating a pervasive awareness, of self and the organization (that is, the culture), that allows one to *pause and self-correct.* In essence, it requires deep, committed self-awareness and personal knowledge.

Warren Bennis, distinguished professor of business at the University of Southern California, found in his research that some of the best leaders stress the importance of *self-knowledge.* He notes, "All of the leaders I talked with agreed that no one can teach you how to become yourself, to take charge, to express yourself, except you."[4(p. 51)] From extensive research on leadership and what makes leaders, Bennis distilled what he calls *The Four Lessons of Self-Knowledge*[4] (*see* Table 1-2, page 5).

Gaining self-knowledge requires openness to change and feedback from external sources and is critically important because we often have inaccurate views of the

Table 1-1. Drucker's Four Competencies

Competency	Description
Listening	"The willingness, ability, and self-discipline to listen" topped Drucker's list. One of the key words is *willingness,* which I consider to be the critical element, because without willingness, no improvement in any aspect of communication—listening or speaking with clarity—can occur.
Clarity	The "willingness to communicate, to make yourself understood," was the next item on Drucker's list. Again, Drucker emphasizes (and so do I) the individual's *willingness* to commit to the communication process and to continually improve communication skills to ensure understanding. Achieving clarity isn't a passive process, especially for leaders.
Accountability	The third item on Drucker's list "is not to alibi yourself." In other words, don't make excuses for yourself or for poor performance, poor outcomes, or substandard safety. Leaders of mettle take responsibility in all situations, success and failure alike. Drucker said that "We either do things to perfection or we don't do them." Sometimes, leaders, especially in health care, need to decide what *not* to be doing . . . not every organization should, for example, do liver transplants or cardiac surgery. Focusing on core competencies and creating unparalleled quality and safety in those competencies, seeking the theoretical ideal of perfection, should be the health care leader's goal.
Stewardship	Drucker's final competency in this short list is to have an "understanding of how unimportant you are when compared to the task." The leader is not the task, and good leaders subordinate themselves to the goal of completing the task. The leader, likewise, is not the organization. Good leaders create an organization that survives even after they depart. Drucker noted that the greatest indictment of a leader is an organization that implodes after the leader leaves. In such circumstances, the leader has failed to create a sustainable vision for the organization. Drucker said leaders needed to be a servant to whatever task the organization required for success. In summary, this is essentially stewardship for the current and future success of the organization.

Source: Adapted from Krames J.A.: *Inside Drucker's Brain.* New York: Portfolio/Penguin, 2008, pp. 201–202.

Table 1-2. Bennis's Four Lessons of Self-Knowledge

Lesson	Description
Learning: You are your own best teacher.	"Learning is experienced as a personal transformation. A person does not gather learnings as possessions but rather becomes a new person,"[4(p. 52)] Bennis states. Experience allows one to adapt to the challenges at hand and lead effectively, even in new situations. Personal transformation occurs with each new learning and each new challenge. Eisenhower communicated this to his son when he spoke of "studious reflection and practice." Experience will teach the willing self-learner.
Accountability: Accept responsibility. Blame no one.	It is your responsibility to be accountable for your learning and self-education. If you are not learning what you need to know, find a way to get the information. Failing to learn falls on the leader's shoulders alone. *Now that the reader has this awareness, he or she is accountable for committing to meaningful change!*
Engagement: You can learn anything you want to learn.	According to Bennis, "If one of the basic ingredients of leadership is a passion for the promises of life, the key to realizing the promise is full deployment of yourself."[4(p. 56)] As the saying goes, if you want to run with the big dogs, you have to get off the porch. I like to think that, when I am reflecting upon my life in old age, I will have thoroughly used up myself and my abilities! This brings to mind a quote sometimes attributed to Hunter S. Thompson that is pervasive now on the Internet: "Life should NOT be a journey to the grave with the intention of arriving safely in an attractive and well preserved body, but rather to skid in sideways, chocolate in one hand, martini in the other, body thoroughly used up, totally worn out."*
Self-Reflection: True understanding comes from reflecting on your experience.	"Reflecting on experience is a means of having a Socratic dialogue with yourself, asking the right questions at the right time, in order to discover the truth of yourself and your life. What really happened? Why did it happen? What did it do to me? What did it mean to me? . . . Nothing is truly yours until you understand it—not even yourself,"[4(p. 56–57)] Bennis says. Again, Eisenhower's words seem prescient.

* Although credited to Thompson, this quote can be found on literally thousands of Web pages, including http://www.43things.com/things/view/913856.

Source: Adapted from Bennis W.: *On Becoming a Leader.* New York: Perseus Books, 2009, pp. 52–57.

way we "are." There is a theory that, in our professional lives, we all have a type of personal hypocrisy at play. This theory, developed by Chris Argyris, states that we have an *espoused theory* of being (how we *claim* to behave) and a *theory in action* (how we *actually* behave—how people actually see us and our behavior).[5] Basically, this theory says we say we think one way when in fact we act another. To those individuals who are around us, this can appear as a lack of integrity. Interestingly, Argyris contends that, as individuals, we are not merely unaware of this discrepancy in our daily lives, but, we are sure it does not exist. This is a frightening combination.

Subsequent work in self-perception by Argyris led to the development of an understanding that there are universal patterns in our professional lives, regardless of occupation, based upon four core values. Argyris contends that we, as individuals, strive to do the following[5]:

1. Remain in control.
2. Win.
3. Suppress negative feelings.
4. Pursue rational objectives.

He argues that because these are values we all hold in our professional life, any suggestion of failure feels like a threat. We avoid threats because of the negative feelings it creates for us, and we "dissociate," or separate, ourselves from anything that will make us feel like we are "losing" or not fulfilling our professional duties.[6] As Quinn states in *Change the World*, "Ironically, we shut down at the exact moment that we most need to be open to learning. In doing so, we begin the process of stagnation, or slow death," in our professional lives.[7(p. 74)]

Most providers will recognize an example of Argyris's four steps of self-rationalization (but will probably associate them with someone else). Think of the last patient you treated who did not improve with your prescribed treatment. There are scenarios in which the four components above might be operating. For illustration, let's imagine that a patient returns to the office several weeks after therapy was initiated but is no better. *Remaining in control* is part of the Argyris equation, and it feels like we are not in control of the situation because there has been no response to our recommended treatment. We like to *win*, but we subconsciously view the failure of the patient to improve as a loss, again because the expectation was that the patient would improve with our recommendation.

Because we *strive to suppress negative feelings,* we *pursue a rationalization* to *suppress the feeling of losing* and think to ourselves that the reason the patient didn't improve is "they were probably noncompliant with our recommendations." Of course, there are other possibilities that we, as individuals, may not want to explore, may not appreciate, or may not even consider as possibilities, such as the fact that we might have missed the diagnosis or prescribed the wrong medicine. Further, our reaction in such a situation may result in losing the patient's respect, with subsequent loss of the patient from our practice. In other words, this line of thinking can impact our business negatively. Sometimes we don't see how our actions in practice impact the business and vice versa. It is a big problem because, as Argyris said, it isn't that we don't see that we are acting this way when it occurs, it is that we know it isn't true.[5]

Self-knowledge requires personal commitment . . . again, *willingness* . . . and this is something that can come only from the individual. And in today's fast-paced world of health care, such personal commitment can seem overwhelming, even unnecessary. Many highly trained individuals feel that leadership is a touchy-feely, intangible quality that is either unimportant or irrelevant to them personally. Such impressions occur at the highest levels of organizations, where those in the C-suite minimize the need and importance of leadership behavior from all individuals, especially providers.

The reader no doubt noted the similarities between Drucker's competencies, Bennis's lessons, and Argyris's perceptions. Accountability for results, whether organizational or personal, is a prominent requirement in each man's list. But at the core of each of these men's work is *the common requirement of an individual's willingness to recognize and commit to the important change* . . . and hard work required to become an effective leader.

The Need for Relationship-Based Civil Leadership

Perspective and age have irrevocably changed my views on leadership. In my first book on leadership—*Applying Personal Leadership to Health Care: The DEPO Principle*—I was intent on making sure physicians understood why effective personal leadership was important and relevant to them on a daily basis. I emphasized that provider behavior was the primary determinant of patient and employee satisfaction and, to the dismay of many, the major driver of malpractice claims. More recently, I have emphasized that shortcomings of personal leadership, especially those around *listening* and *clarity* of communication, create the majority—*yes, the majority*—of patient quality and safety concerns. My presentations to health care organizations and providers have echoed these messages over and over.

Much to my amazement, the message has often been lost on the audience. Some physicians—sometimes a majority—have denied that leadership is relevant to them. More aggressive audiences—also often a majority—have enjoyed pointing out "You don't even practice medicine anymore . . . how could you possibly understand what we are going through?!" (At the time, I was developing leadership materials and doing training, and I was not in active practice.) Somewhat to my surprise, apparently after a physician quits active practice, he or she forgets everything about having actually been in practice, good or bad! In other words, individuals sought ways to self-justify (remember Argyris), not adhering to basic principles of civil behavior. . . . I was apparently unaware that one must be a practicing physician to demonstrate qualities such as respect, empathy, and honesty. In brief, the audiences of health care providers (mainly physicians) have not seemed able or willing to see the link between their behavior and their careers. They have not seen that leadership is, in fact, an outward manifestation of their behavior, good or bad, effective or not. Behavior is the visible manifestation of an individual's character and competence. Behavior is how character and competence are translated into action.

Because of the challenge of communicating the importance of leadership to the health care profession, I struggled with how such a message should be communicated to create understanding, and, to use an over-used term, establish "buy-in." It hit me in May of 2006, when I participated in the International Association of Protocol Consultants (IAPC) conference in Washington, D.C. Dr. P. M. Forni, who wrote a book titled *Choosing Civility: The Twenty-Five Rules of Considerate Conduct,* gave one of the presentations.[8]

After hearing Dr. Forni's presentation, I realized that I needed to stop talking about leadership and start speaking to health care providers about *civility.* According to Dr. Forni, civility is a code of behavior based on *respect, restraint,* and *responsibility.* It was an epiphany for me, as it occurred to me that no one—even physicians— with any modicum of self-perspective would stand up in an audience and proclaim, "Civility isn't relevant to me." Yet the Principles of Civility are nearly identical to those of leadership, resulting in a happy coincidence for my message and me.

Cherlynn Conetsco, also a presenter at the IAPC meeting that year, has trained many military attachés who represent the United States abroad in the six Principles of Civility[9]:

1. Respect
2. Empathy
3. Flexibility
4. Interest in other cultures
5. Tolerance
6. Technical skills

The Principles of Civility should be core, *expected* behaviors of all health care workers. Listening effectively and communicating with clarity in health care requires the Principles of Civility . . . especially respect and empathy. These two principles are absolute requirements for a health care provider. Can you imagine a provider who doesn't listen being perceived by the patient or family as ineffective and uncaring? Can you imagine a cancer patient listening to a provider giving them dire information with clarity but delivered with coldness and distance? Of course, you can imagine these things, but it isn't what *you* would want to experience as an individual, is it? The Principles of Civility provide important depth to Drucker's and Bennis's leadership concepts, especially as they relate to health care provider leadership. Whether leading your own office practice or a larger organization, civil leadership is paramount and results from the nexus of Drucker's competencies, Bennis's self-knowledge, and the Principles of Civility.

Importantly, civil leadership isn't just a nice way of being, it is a *critical business strategy,* as will be discussed at length later in the book. Organizations that prescribe to civil leadership as a basic, *enforced* organizational expectation will gain a huge competitive market advantage in the next 30 years. They will be able to effectively attract and retain the best employees and providers and have the highest-quality outcomes, unparalleled patient safety and satisfaction, and lowest personal and organizational liability. Perhaps most importantly, the organization and those within it will feel good about themselves. Now *that's* a stewardship legacy I would like as a leader!

So now what? We can't simply send someone off to a leadership institute and have them come back the ideal leader? No. But we can teach the key principles of listening, clarity of communication, accountability, stewardship, and using civility's principles as a touchstone, and through practice and the development of self-knowledge—actually applying what we learn in specific situations—we can develop the ability to consistently lead with success and *civility* when challenged, regardless of environment.

Leadership Is Situational, Civility Isn't

The situational nature of leadership is a major theme of this book. Effective leadership is *situational* . . . in other words, even in the most complex of situations, a leader doesn't have to be "on" all of the time. It seems that effective leadership occurs in brief (although perhaps frequent or even daily) spurts of decision making or rallying of the troops, so to speak. In other words, a leader doesn't have to manifest leadership 24/7/365. What a leader must manifest all day, every day, however, is civility, because civility is—or at least should be—an expectation of all of us . . . even in health care.

The issue of not taking the time to become a better leader or a better communicator (that is, being *willing*), especially in light of what it means to patient safety and outcome, is a common challenge of health care providers, administrators, and their organizations. "I'm too busy" is an oft-heard comment. It is like a marathon runner saying, "I'm too busy running to take time for a drink!" during the race. In the end, willing commitment to improvement is an issue of *accountability for self,* one of Drucker's key leadership qualities. Giovinella Gonthier and Kevin Morrissey tell us that civility is also dependent on the individual's willingness:

> *The ultimate responsibility rests on our individual shoulders to behave in a civil manner and promote that kind of behavior in others. We must look beyond the culture of blame ("It's not my fault!") and honestly appraise what we are really about and what type of individuals we want to be. Do we really have so many demands on our time in the 21st century that we have to give up accountability?* [10(p. 21)]

How do we know that we are not meeting the expectations of civil behavior in our lives and our organizations? We must *self-monitor ourselves.* As Robert E. Quinn, distinguished professor of Organizational Behavior and Human Resource Management at the University of Michigan Business School, notes in his book *Change the World: How Ordinary People Can Accomplish Extraordinary Results,* we know we are acting with integrity *by monitoring our own behavior for episodes that lack integrity.*[11] Civil leadership isn't about perfection. Rather, it is about creating personal and organizational expectations regarding civil behaviors and then monitoring ourselves. When we detect that we have violated what we expect of ourselves or from those within our organization, we self-correct by apologizing, if necessary, or redirecting our efforts in a more positive direction.

The preceding discussion throws my perhaps overly simplistic assertion about formulaic leadership into sharp relief against the backdrop of those who might have us believe otherwise. If excellent leadership requires that one learn *The Four Lessons of Self-Knowledge* to attain maximally effective leadership in the context of civility, by definition then, effective leadership *cannot* be taught to another because it is largely *self-learned* by motivated, willing individuals! Effective leaders are effective because they make their own life by *understanding it in the context of a basic skill set, experience, and self-analysis.* President Eisenhower's leadership, then, is not reproducible. He once alluded to this by noting: "unlike Presidential administrations, problems rarely have terminal dates."[12] While his point was that the ongoing nature of our country's problems outlives a president's tenure, another interpretation is that his solutions would not be the same as those of the next administration. Think Bush versus Obama. Wow! Each leader brings his or her perspective and life experience to bear on challenges, with different results and different degrees of success. While all effective leaders must have Drucker's four competencies and behave with civility, no leader brings someone else's self-knowledge! It is unique to each individual, rendering leadership formulas impotent.

Gosh, It Sounds Good, But . . .

Most readers will agree with what has been written thus far, but real, meaningful, sustained change is a very different commitment for providers. While you can personally have the willingness to commit to the competencies, a path of self-knowledge, and the Principles of Civility, resistance at the organizational level is ensured if you intend to drive cultural change based on this model.

Quinn has observed that people resist in a predictable sequence when confronted with new, potentially transformational ideas proposed by "change agents" (that is, individuals). *First,* Quinn says, people will laugh at the new idea; however, when they see that the change agent isn't laughing, they subsequently move to the *second defensive strategy* of providing one hundred and one reasons why the idea won't work—rationalizations. The *third* and final step for those who wish to continue to resist the change agent is to resort to "moral indignation," calling into question the individual's motives, morals, qualifications, ethics, or abilities in order to maintain the status quo or defend the current system.[11] (Remember the common audience response I received in physician leadership presentation? "You don't even practice!") The reason for these visceral responses is related to the current culture, whatever it may be, and defines the environment in which the people being asked to change operate. The suggestion that the culture of health care needs to be changed is extraordinarily threatening because it redefines the expectations of people within the profession. People no longer know how to act, what their responsibilities are, and how to play by the rules. Part of the challenge in changing the environment in health care is that inappropriate, uncivil behavior has long been tolerated and gone uncorrected. Complaints, even through the proper chain of command, can result in retaliation, subtle or overt, that stifles further interest in trying to create what so many really want: civility. Perhaps even worse are complaints that are found valid through follow-up, yet where no consequences are meted out to the offender. These experiences communicate to those within the organization that the leaders are not serious about meaningful change. What you permit, you promote.

In the end, the reader cannot argue that the concepts I present are inaccurate, untrue, or not relevant to each individual health care provider. A common response of providers, especially successful physicians, is that "it isn't relevant to my world." They might say they "live in the real world," and these principles and concepts don't apply. Quinn points out that what people really mean to say in circumstances where major change is proposed is that the suggested change is *too hard* or requires *too much sacrifice* on their part. The change I am speaking of in this book won't be easy, and I clearly and openly acknowledge that fact. Quinn points out: "If one person can do this, it destroys the credibility of the universal argument, 'But you do not understand. . . .'"[11]

It is important to understand, as individuals desiring civil leadership, that all we need to do is reach out and grab what is in front of us . . . to be *willing to commit* to what is needed. Acting with civility is within everyone's reach, as are the competencies and self-knowledge of effective leadership. As Parker Palmer so eloquently reminds us:

> *. . . no punishment anyone lays on you could possibly be worse than the*

punishment you lay on yourself by conspiring in your own diminishment. With that insight comes the ability to open cell doors that were never locked in the first place and to walk into new possibilities that honor the claims of one's heart. [13(p. 178)]

It is time for providers and their organizations to walk through the open door of relationship-based civil leadership.

Chapter Summary

- Peter Drucker, the most influential management theorist of the twentieth century, believed that leadership could be boiled down to four competencies: *listening, clarity of communication, accountability,* and *stewardship* for the current and future success of the organization.

- Achieving and maintaining Drucker's four competencies requires that an individual be committed to developing what Warren Bennis calls self-knowledge—a deep understanding of oneself, developed through learning, accountability, engagement, and self-reflection.

- The Principles of Civility—*respect, empathy, flexibility, interest in other cultures, tolerance,* and *technical skills*—provide the context for developing the competencies and seeking self-knowledge, in order to develop the civil leadership skills critical to the success of health care providers and their organization's future.

References

1. Westley F., Mintzberg H.: Visionary leadership and strategic management. *Strategic Management Journal* 10:17–32, 1989.
2. Ambrose S.E.: *The Supreme Commander: The War Years of General Dwight D. Eisenhower.* Jackson, MS: University Press of Mississippi, 1999.
3. Krames J.A.: *Inside Drucker's Brain.* New York: Portfolio/Penguin, 2008.
4. Bennis W.: *On Becoming a Leader.* New York: Perseus Books, 2009.
5. Argyris C.: Crafting a theory of practice: The case of organizational paradoxes. In Quinn R.E., Camerson K.S. (eds.): *Paradox and Transformation: Toward a Theory of Change in Organization and Management.* Cambridge, MA: Ballinger, 1988, pp. 255–278.
6. Argyris C.: Teaching smart people how to learn. *Harvard Business Review* 69:99–109, May–Jun. 1991.
7. Quinn R.E.: *Change the World: How Ordinary People Can Accomplish Extraordinary Results.* San Francisco: Jossey-Bass, 2000.
8. Forni P.M.: Choosing civility. Lecture given at the International Association of Protocol Consultants conference, Washington, DC, May 5–7, 2006.

9. Conetsco C.: Mastering protocol, etiquette, & civility. Presented at the International Association of Protocol Consultants conference, Washington DC, May 5–7, 2006.

10. Gonthier G., Morrissey K.: *Rude Awakenings: Overcoming the Civility Crisis in the Workplace.* Chicago: Dearborn Trade Publishing, 2002.

11. Personal communication between the author and Robert E. Quinn on his book *Change the World.*

12. Eisenhower D.: State of the Union Address, Jan. 12, 1961. http://www.presidency.ucsb.edu/ws/index.php?pid=12074 (accessed Jun. 27, 2009).

13. Palmer P.: *The Courage to Teach: Exploring the Inner Landscape of a Teacher's Life.* San Francisco: Jossey-Bass, 2007.

Chapter Two
The Self-Inflicted Injuries of Disruptive and Uncivil Behavior

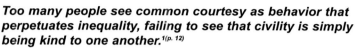

Too many people see common courtesy as behavior that perpetuates inequality, failing to see that civility is simply being kind to one another.[1(p. 12)]
—Giovinella Gonthier and Kevin Morrissey

Civility conjures up images of some Emily Post–like formal set of rules of etiquette regarding personal behavior in public. But in reality it is simply an overall concern about treating others—all others—in a reasonable, respectful, empathetic manner. Conversely, incivility is, simply put, inappropriate or bad behavior characterized by lack of consideration for others.[1] Incivility is manifest by verbal, physical, or other nonverbal patterns of behavior. Gonthier and Morrissey have assembled a list of examples of incivility in the workplace, and I include them here because it gives the provider perspective about what is considered incivility in a business environment (*see* Box 2-1, page 16).[1] Why is this relevant? Because repeated acts of incivility are the basis for terminating an employee in most industries. The health care industry benchmarks itself in terms of safety and outcome but has not benchmarked itself to the higher standards of behavior found in other industries. It is time we do.

The *New York Times* published a story in 2008 titled "Arrogant, Abusive and Disruptive—And a Doctor," highlighting many aspects of incivility in health care perpetrated by physicians.[2] The author chronicles a nurse who had been brought to "tears so many times that she was trying to start her own business and leave nursing."[2(p. D1)] The article speaks of a study of 102 nonprofit hospitals in which two thirds of survey respondents noted *a link between disruptive behavior and medical mistakes.* Nearly 20% of respondents said they knew of an error that resulted from a disruptive physician. The author goes on to describe a study by the Institute for Safe Medication Practices which found that 4 out of 10 hospital staff members kept their mouth shut about medication orders they felt were incorrect because they didn't want to confront the physician. In 7% of those cases, staff knew their silence actually contributed to medication errors. In virtually any other industry that

Box 2-1. Examples of Workplace Incivility

- Not returning phone calls, voice mails, or e-mails
- Shouting at someone, regardless of status
- Berating underlings in public
- Removing someone's area of responsibility without consulting him or her
- Belittling people who are different or think differently from you
- Habitually interrupting others
- Acting as though only your opinions count
- Setting impossible deadlines for your subordinates to meet
- Not recognizing everyone's strength in a group project
- Failing to acknowledge colleagues in the hallway
- Not keeping appointments
- Permanently replacing a woman who is on maternity leave with another worker

Source: Gonthier G., Morrissey K.: *Rude Awakenings: Overcoming the Civility Crisis in the Workplace.* Chicago: Dearborn Trade Publishing, 2002, p. 25.

comes to mind, this type of behavior, especially associated with errors or employee loss, would result in the perpetrator being fired.

The article relates other stories—one about a resident who was afraid to call the attending physician, who was known to yell and ridicule residents. The result: a dead baby. Or the story about the surgeon, who got upset at a nurse, telling her to "just get the patient ready." After then operating on the wrong side, he yelled at the entire operating team. His message: "Not my fault. You should have prevented this." Never mind the fact that he had not cooperated with them in the standardized preoperative process.

The data that tell us that bad behavior—uncivil behavior—drives down health care quality and worsens patient safety are undeniable. And the kinds of behavior observed in the situations described above—include belittling, insulting, or yelling, often in front of patients or other staff—are certainly addressed in Box 2-1. Simply put, the reason to act with civility is more than just to "be nice." Quality and safety depend on it.

Civility in health care leadership is not a new concept, just one that has to be revisited. In 1873, at a conference of superintendents of psychiatric hospitals, Dr. Isaac Ray, Butler Hospital's first CEO, presented a paper, "Ideal Characters of the Officers of a Hospital for the Insane," in which he described "The Good Superintendent" and "The Good Director." The paragons displayed included the following[3]:

- Respect for other physicians and for patients
- Nonjudgmental listening skills
- Willingness to subordinate one's ego to the service of humanity
- Personal accountability
- Immersion in and knowledge of the day-to-day workings of the hospital and its staff
- Support and encouragement of physicians

It seems all we need to do is live with Dr. Ray's character list from more than 100 years ago!

For the better part of a decade, I have promoted physician leadership as a key to health care's ills—plummeting patient satisfaction, malpractice costs spiraling out of control, patient safety violations, and health care practitioners discouraging young people from entering a profession that can be rewarding in ways others cannot.[4] I now believe the key to health care's challenges is more basic and understandable than leadership. The key is civility from and between providers, patients, families, administrators, and even attorneys—in other words, relationship-based care. Behaving with civility is, in essence, good personal leadership, and it is essential for those who lead others.

Other physicians seem to be beginning to understand what I have been preaching during the decade. Michael Kahn, M.D., recently noted that "medical schools may be underemphasizing a much simpler virtue: good manners."[5(p. D6)] He describes six steps to "etiquette-based medicine," including introducing yourself, shaking hands, sitting down with a patient, and smiling. He notes that patients derive comfort from such actions. Certainly these things fall within the realm of civility.

Just about the most important thing we do in life is interact with other human beings—spouse, children, parents, friends, coworkers—and, in health care, patients and their families. P. M. Forni notes, "a crucial measure of our success in life is the way we treat one another every day of our lives."[6(p. 4)] As providers, we interact with patients who feel vulnerable and afraid. The relationship skills of health care providers determine the quality of the health care experience for all involved, whether patient, nurse, aid, physician, or pharmacist.

At first blush, the need for civility may seem obscure. Closer examination, however, leads one to the undeniable conclusion that civility is the key to transforming health care. Unfortunately, common knowledge does not automatically result in common practice. As Dr. Forni eloquently states, we all have equilibrium. We all have balance, but that doesn't mean one who has never been on a bike can simply get on and pedal off. We all have the ability to float in water but must learn to swim. We can all speak, but we may not be understood—we may not communicate effectively. To use a computer analogy, we all are made with hardware to run the civility "program" but may have loaded the wrong software (that is, learned less-than-civil behavior). Physicians, especially, may run the wrong software, downloaded during training—and much of our behavior is learned during training.

The reader needs to understand that patients and their families are passive observers of their surroundings in health care organizations. They see the actions and interactions of the staff within the hospital or clinic. They see uncivil treatment of nursing staff by physicians. They see senior nurses verbally abuse and bully their young preceptors. They see behavior that should demand an apology go without so much as a compassionate look, much less an "I'm sorry." They surely wonder why professional people—who are supposed to embody the very concepts of compassion, empathy, and respect—can't even treat each other with the common civility afforded someone with whom they accidentally bump into while walking on the street. What program are we running?

Breaking Down the Six Principles of Civility
The six Principles of Civility, as noted previously, are respect, empathy, flexibility, interest in other cultures, tolerance, and technical skills. It shouldn't be a big surprise that these principles significantly overlap with Drucker's competencies and optimally require Bennis's commitment to self-knowledge. It also should be no surprise that they form not only the basis of civil leadership but also of relationship-based care.

Respect is like air: It's often more noticeable in its absence than in its presence. Deny someone respect, and that person will have difficulty thinking about anything else. If you've ever witnessed the difference in care provided by respected staff and by those who are the object of a physician's disdain or contempt, you know everything you need to know about the significance of respect in staff motivation and performance.

Empathy, the ability to understand and share the feelings of another—such as fear, anxiety, or pain—is critical for health care providers. What is the one commonality all providers share with each other and the patient? Humanity. And therein lies the ground from which empathy springs: Empathy is the very basis of our profession.

Flexibility is mandatory when one deals with living, breathing beings. I have a saying that "Life is DUN." Life is not linear and logical. Rather it is dynamic, unpredictable, and nonlinear. If we are not flexible, disappointment will be our constant companion. And disappointment tends to "trickle down": Your disenchantment can easily become someone else's, and so forth.

Interest in other cultures is a subset of common curiosity. A different hue of skin or contrasting vocal accent can be a springboard to learning for the interested—or an impediment (or worse) for the unconcerned. One cannot be a citizen in the twenty-first century without having an interest in other cultures. Respect married to an interest in other cultures is a recipe for a successful practice in ethnically diverse countries such as the United States, Great Britain, Canada, and France and many other Western European countries.

Tolerance is a clear descendant of the first four principles. Tolerance isn't "embracing"; it's recognizing, respecting, and allowing for differences—between people, ideas, and actions.

Technical skills don't include wielding a scalpel or administering an MRI. They aren't even solely the physicians' ability to diagnose and treat. Communication is a skill—it can and *must* be learned—and it may be the most significant technical resource a physician can employ. Communication is a *learned* skill, and one that we in health care have woefully neglected to the detriment of our patients, employees, and safe, high-quality health care. It is also one of the Drucker competencies, whose importance is grossly underestimated in health care. When one becomes aware of the relevance of unclear communication and the effect on health care quality and patient safety as well as provider liability, competencies of listening and clarity take on vital importance. One operating group of The Doctors Company, one of the largest U.S. medical malpractice insurers, reviewed closed claims to identify the drivers of malpractice claims. In 47% of the reviewed cases, some form of communication failure or misfire was identified.[7] More than 64% of the 2,090 adverse events reported to The Joint Commission between July 2006 and June 2009 had communication identified as a root cause.[8]

Providers might ponder why the Principles of Civility are important. After all, most providers I know would claim that they act with civility on a daily basis. Reality tells us differently: We often don't know what we don't know.

Consider the data that tell us civility is a problem, and consider that there are clear social and personal benefits to acting with civility:

Civility Is Connected to the Principle of Respect for Other People

A civil individual treats all others as ends in themselves, as intrinsically valuable individuals, rather than as those who serve some immediate need or desire. The latter is, in essence, a form of slavery. In health care, a common observation is seeing physicians treat nurses and other providers as tools of patient care rather than as valued team members. Such treatment is disrespectful and runs counter to the team-based care approach that has been demonstrated to be superior to traditional physician-centric care.

There Is a Connection Between Incivility, Business Results, and Violence

In the everyday workplace, acts of disrespect are spiraling out of control. More than 45% of respondents in a survey of 800 people conducted by the University of North Carolina at Chapel Hill's Kenan-Flagler Business School, contemplated a job changes because of rudeness, and 12% actually changed jobs.[9]

A good number of violent incidents have been linked to incivility in the workplace. What's this got to do with health care? Of 1,200 individuals interviewed, 30% knew of a nurse who had quit his or her job due to the behavior of a physician.

The cost to health care organizations in turnover costs related to provider behavior is horrific, estimated in 1997 dollars to be $150,000 per disruptive physician.[9] This translates into $200,000 in 2009 dollars![10]

Further, the data strongly suggest that physician violations of the principles of respect and empathy are the major generators of medical malpractice claims. Multiple small violations of trust by the physician—habitually being late in the clinic, telling patients they will call with lab results and failing to do so, interrupting, limiting questions or controlling the conversation during the office visit, and failing to apologize for the various violations of civility—create conditions that lead patients to sue when an outcome is less than expected. Patients are angry at the physician *before* the outcome that leads them to sue. The unexpected outcome is simply the proverbial straw that breaks the camel's back, leading the angry person to sue.

There Is a Connection Between Civility and Personal Well-Being

The quality of our personal lives depends on the quality of our relationships with others, but the quality of our relationships depends on our relational skills. The six Principles of Civility serve as our guide for how to behave toward our fellow humans. Each principle can be learned and cultivated, if we are open to self-examination and honest feedback from those around us. And to reiterate, acting with civility is not situational.

Data specific to incivility and health care will be presented in greater detail in Chapter 6.

Only by committing to the Principles of Civility can health care providers be more effective in what they strive to do in the first place: care for others. The Principles of Civility are critical to catapulting us over the hurdles we face in health care, leaving them far behind in the mist of the past; understanding them requires only that one be a human being. Acting with civility doesn't require an M.D., R.N., or any other degree. It is a beautiful reality that being this way also happens to result in improved safety and quality, lower liability, and greater satisfaction throughout the system. Marrying the Principles of Civility to Drucker's competencies and Bennis's self-knowledge provides a powerful platform for industry change, led by the providers who are ready to take health care to the next level.

It's Not About Perfection

Often my stake-in-the-ground position about civility is, perhaps, misinterpreted as a cry for adhering to the Principles of Civility with nothing short of perfection . . . that one should, in every circumstance, act unfailingly with civility. It is important for me to emphasize that I am not speaking of perfection. Instead, I am hoping to help the reader create a *personal self-awareness* that leads each to pause and reflect when acting in a way that is *not* civil. It is in the reflection that, as Quinn and Bennis point out, we realize gaps in our behavior, and subsequently make appropriate changes, and, if necessary, reparations or apologies, as the situation may require.

To illustrate, let me give you two examples, with a small—but critical—nuance in the story. I will use myself as the example in this fictitious story.

Story One

Imagine that I have been up all night long on general surgery and trauma call. I have admitted four patients and done two surgeries. In addition, I fielded multiple phone calls, including one for a change in the pain medicine for Mrs. Wilson, who had become confused on hydromorphone. I changed the medicine to morphine. On rounds several hours later, I am reviewing the chart and notice that the phone order was not written and that Mrs. Wilson received several more doses of hydromorphone. I track down the charge nurse, Susan. I ask angrily, with furrowed brows, "What's going on here? I was called last night about this and changed this to morphine. Why wasn't this changed?" Susan responds "I don't know, Dr. Woods." I then raise my voice to a near-yell and say, "I can't believe this! It is inexcusable!" as I throw the chart on the workstation and storm off down the hall, muttering angrily under my breath. Multiple people—other nurses, aides, patients, and family members—witness this. Few act as if they are paying attention, staring at the chart in front of them, but everyone is acutely aware of what happened . . . and they are intimidated and perhaps even scared.

Story Two

Now imagine that Story One occurs as described above, in exactly the same manner. But as I turn to storm off down the hall, something in my head—*my own desire for civility, my self-awareness, the knowledge of organizational expectations for behavior, and the training I have had in the competencies*—makes me pause and stop in my tracks. I bow my head and scratch it embarrassingly, and think for a moment, staring at the floor. The nurses, aides, patients, and family members are still watching, holding their breath, as I slowly turn around and sheepishly say, "Susan, just a moment. I'm sorry for my outburst just now. I was up all night, and I am just crabby, but that isn't an excuse for how I just treated you. Again, I'm sorry. It won't happen again." I turn and walk away with humility. Everyone witnessing the scene feels a sense of relief and gratitude for working in a place where civility is the touchstone for daily operations, and self-correction and apology is the norm.

The tone of this second story is characterized by the ability of the individual to self-monitor his behavior—not demanding perfection of self or others but rather recognizing that he violated the Principles of Civility, civil leadership, and plain common courtesy. The recognition allowed self-correction, and everyone who witnessed this scene had a very different, in fact positive, impression of the events and the physician. Interactions like the ones just illustrated set the tone of a unit and, in fact, an entire organization.

When an organization publically commits to the concepts of civil leadership, things become more interesting. Saying you believe something is one thing. Getting the organization—that is, the individuals within the organization—to actually live with the tenants of civil leadership is another. It is far better to not publically declare commitment to a path of civility than to proclaim it is your path and not follow through, because doing so will result in cynical employees and staff. Not enforcing expectations for civil behavior in an organization generates cynicism through a low-trust, ineffective culture that self-perpetuates. Stephen Covey notes:

> *This [organizational] misalignment will manifest itself in a thousand ways, contributing to even lower trust and more politicized behavior and interdepartmental rivalries. Rules will take the place of human judgment because as things get out of hand, managers will feel the need for increased control. Bureaucracy, hierarchies, rules and regulations will become like* prostheses *for trust. Any talk of people or leadership development will be considered soft, "touchy-feely," unrealistic, wasteful and costly. People, like things, will become an expense, not an investment.*[11(p. 108)]

I suspect many readers will recognize this in their own organization, whether superior or subordinate. If you are one of them, this is your wake-up call!

Chapter Summary

- Incivility in the workplace is characterized by lack of consideration for others and can be displayed verbally, physically, and in other nonverbal ways.
- Etiquette-based medicine—such as introducing oneself, shaking hands, sitting down, and smiling—provides comfort to patients in sometimes uncomfortable circumstances.
- The six Principles of Civility—*respect, empathy, flexibility, interest in other cultures, tolerance,* and *technical skills*—are the foundation of both civil leadership and relationship-based care.
- The marriage of the Principles of Civility, Drucker's competencies (*listening, clarity, accountability,* and *stewardship*), and Bennis's concept of self-knowledge (*learning, accountability, engagement,* and *self-reflection*) give leaders an arsenal for powerful industry change.

References

1. Gonthier G., Morrissey K.: *Rude Awakenings: Overcoming the Civility Crisis in the Workplace.* Chicago: Dearborn Trade Publishing, 2002.
2. Tarkan L.: Arrogant, abusive and disruptive—And a doctor. *New York Times* p. D1, Dec. 2, 2008.
3. Recupero P.R., Rainey S.E.: The ideal physician executive. *Med Health R I* 89:232–235, Jul. 2006.
4. Woods M.S.: *Applying Personal Leadership Skills to Healthcare: The DEPO Principle.* Tampa, FL: ACPE Press, 2001.
5. Kahn M.: The six habits of highly respectful physicians. *New York Times* p. D6 Dec. 2, 2008.
6. Forni P.M.: *Choosing Civility: The Twenty-Five Rules of Considerate Conduct.* New York: St. Martin's Press, 2002.
7. Conversation between the author and Darrell Ranum, vice president, Risk Management, The Doctors Company/OHIC Insurance, Feb. 19, 2008.
8. Personal correspondence between the author and The Joint Commission Office of Quality Monitoring, Sep. 24, 2009.
9. Pfifferling J.H.: Managing the unmanageable: The disruptive physician. *Fam Pract Manag* 4:76–78, 83, 87–92, Nov.–Dec. 1997.
10. Data derived from The Inflation Calculator, http://www.westegg.com/inflation/ (accessed Feb. 5, 2010).
11. Covey, S.R.: *The 8th Habit: From Effectiveness to Greatness.* New York: Free Press, 2004.

Chapter Three
Relationship-Based Civil Leadership as a Health Care Business Strategy

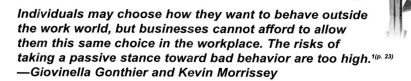

Individuals may choose how they want to behave outside the work world, but businesses cannot afford to allow them this same choice in the workplace. The risks of taking a passive stance toward bad behavior are too high.[1(p. 23)]
—*Giovinella Gonthier and Kevin Morrissey*

The Costs of Incivility (Bad Behavior)

All of the behaviors one associates with civility are critical to establishing effective working relationships with colleagues, patients, and health care staff. Civil leadership—that is, good behavior—has a direct effect on health care outcomes (compliance and safety), satisfaction, and malpractice liability. Behavior of individuals in leadership positions, whether a formal or informal position of leadership (power), has profound effects on employee satisfaction and retention, each of which can impact the organization's bottom line. Consider these points, which cut across all groups of health care providers:

- In a survey of nurses, pharmacists, and physicians, 30% of respondents knew of a nurse who left an organization because of disruptive physician behaviors.[2]
- Hostile treatment of graduate nurses by more senior nurses results in high staff turnover, and the resultant poor communication results in poorer patient care.[3]
- Sixty percent of new nurses leave their first job within six months due to nurse-on-nurse violence . . . primarily verbal abuse from the individual's *preceptor.* Twenty percent of new nurses leave the profession of nursing within three years to escape hostility.[3]
- Disruptive behaviors of both nurses and physicians have a documented significant negative effect on patient outcomes.[2]
- High-stress areas in medicine, such as the operating room, are bastions of dysfunction that dramatically inhibit optimal team function and reduce the likelihood of an optimal outcome. One survey found that "Disruptive behaviors increased levels of stress and frustration, which impaired concentration, impeded communication flow, and adversely affected staff relationships and team collaboration. These events were perceived to increase the likelihood of medical errors and adverse events and to compromise patient safety and quality of care."[4(p. 96)]

Companies of all flavors spend millions of dollars annually on leadership and communications training for their employees. This isn't done out of the goodness of their hearts; they do it because such training has time and again demonstrated *huge* returns on a company's investment. Improvements realized from focused enhancement of leadership skills have a beneficial effect on the organization for years beyond the initial training, with sustained improvements in customer and employee loyalty and organizational profitability. Providers, their practices, and health care organizations can realize the same benefits of leadership and communications training, yet few health care organizations see the value proposition. Such expense is viewed as promoting "fluffy, touchy-feely" stuff, not as the critical business proposition it really is.

Relationship-based civil leadership, along with the attendant improved communication and interpersonal skills, will increase health care revenue in five distinct, often-underappreciated areas:

1. *Increased patient satisfaction and retention.* Few physicians or health care organizations realize that attracting new patients costs six times as much as keeping the ones they have by ensuring that they are satisfied. Further, a 5% increase in customer retention translates into a 25%–125% increase in revenue![5]

2. *Increased health care employee satisfaction and reduced turnover.* I have consulted with health care organizations that have 18%–27% annual turnover of their health care staff, including nurses, resulting in millions of dollars of lost revenue annually. Providers do not appreciate that replacement and retraining costs for an employee are estimated to be between 70% and 200% of the departing employee's annual income.[6] If a health care organization (or provider) decreases employee turnover, it can also decrease its costs.

3. *Reduced provider malpractice premiums.* As a result of enhanced patient and employee satisfaction, as well as increased physician personal effectiveness, communication, and interpersonal skills, malpractice liability will decrease. Civility Mutual Educational Services, of which I am the founder, actually suggests that groups of physicians ask for premium discounts if they demonstrate an overall improvement in civil leadership skills through a documented, standardized approach.

4. *Reduced health care organizational liability.* A significant degree of stress within health care cultures is driven by provider behavior. In a study of 12,000 health care workers, examining how job stress affected medical malpractice risks, organizations in which workers had the greatest number of complaints concerning on-the-job stress had the highest rates of medical malpractice claims.

Providers who create stress due to their behavior contribute to stress within an institution, resulting in an *unnecessary* increase in organizational liability.[7-10]

5. ***Enhanced quality outcomes and patient safety.*** Better communication and patient rapport translate into better treatment compliance, with fewer complications and better health outcomes.[11,12] In this day of pay-for-performance, quality equals dollars. In capitated environments, enhanced compliance results in fewer dollars being spent from the kitty—for the right reasons. You simply keep more of what you are paid.

The Bottom-Line Cost of Losing Employees

Every provider interacts with other staff and patients. It is crucial that providers treat both with civility—with respect, empathy, and compassion—to achieve the critical strategic goal of retaining valuable employees and patients: in other words, providing civility-driven, relationship-based health care. Doing so will directly affect the practice's success. A physician who enables employee satisfaction and motivation will reduce employee stress and turnover within the organization. And reduced turnover decreases the amount of time and money spent trying to attract and retrain replacements. Further, reducing stress in health care employees is statistically correlated to reducing organizational malpractice risk.[7]

Health care organizations—and their providers—often don't appreciate the huge expense associated with losing an employee. How expensive is employee turnover? Recruitment and retraining costs to replace a single departing employee range from 1.5 to 2 times the departing employee's annual salary.[13] Children's Hospital of Pittsburgh reported an average cost of $17,486 to replace a single staff member in its poison control center.[14] This pales in comparison to what it costs to replace an unhappy physician who leaves a health care organization. Recruitment and replacement costs for a single primary care physician run $236,383 for a general/family practice physician, $245,128 for a general internist, and $264,383 for a pediatrician. The total turnover costs for the 533 physicians studied in these groups tracked over a five-year period was $69 million.[15]

In the June 2002 *American Journal of Nursing,* VHA West health system reported that of 1,200 nurses, administrators, and physicians surveyed, 93% had witnessed disruptive physician behavior.[16] Nearly one third knew of at least one nurse who had quit his or her job because of a physician's behavior. Such unprofessional behavior should not be tolerated in any organization. But it also costs money:

Some estimate that a single disruptive physician can cost an organization $150,000 per year in employee turnover. This is lost income—money physicians and their organizations never recover or realize as income.

"Turnover in the health care industry is a major detriment to the delivery of cost-efficient, quality care," according to Kiel.[17(p. 12)] Satisfied employees, on the other hand—especially nurses—increase patient satisfaction and improve patient outcomes, resulting in retained or increased dollars for the practice or organization.

Lest one scoff at the importance of ensuring employee satisfaction in health care as a strategic focus for organizational success, consider this: The current and future prosperity of a health care organization is contingent on its ability to find, train, and retain a high-quality staff, especially nurses.[18] With nearly 60% of the current nursing force over the age of 40 years, combined with the fact that the number of R.N.s under the age of 30 years has fallen nearly 40%, medical offices and hospitals will have to scramble for a limited talent pool, and they may be doing so already.[19] It stands to reason that the total number of R.N.s will shrink even further after 2010, when substantial portions of the "baby-boomer" nurses retire. Retention of talented nonphysician health care employees should be a primary strategic goal of medical organizations and will determine whether they survive, much less compete, in the next two decades. Provider behavior and leadership will have a direct effect on the success of this strategy.

In a 2008 *Wall Street Journal* article titled "Keeping Workers Earns a Bonus in Some Offices," Cari Tuna noted that some firms view employee retention as such an important key to organizational success that managers are incentivized by bonuses to reduce employee turnover.[20] Roger S. Penske of Penske Automotive Group was paid a $240,000 bonus for reducing attrition to 30.8%—a mere 0.4% improvement over the year previous! While this may seem excessive, it highlights the importance organizations are placing on retention and the expense related to employee churn and organizational profitability. Imagine what incentivizing a nursing manager—based on unit retention . . . or a whole unit whose bonus is tied to it—would mean for turnover!

Why Relationship-Based Civil Leadership Is Good Business Strategy

Some may remain skeptical of the value of leadership training in health care, but there are clear, evidence-based examples of leadership's value. Undeniable statistical confirmation of leadership's value came in late 2001. David Maister published *Practice What You Preach,* a book based on a prospective, longitudinal study of the major organizational influences that determine financial performance.[21] Maister's hypothesis was that when leaders are effective as individuals and energize and excite their employees, employees will better serve customers. As a result of excellent service, the clients will be more loyal, and loyalty produces more revenue for the organization.

Maister tested this hypothesis in 139 offices in 15 countries in 15 different industries. This is not exactly a small sample size, and it absolutely meets the definition of "evidence based," which we are so fond of invoking in health care. Maister examined four objective measures of organizational financial performance, obtained from each of the offices:

1. Two-year percentage growth in profits
2. Two-year percentage growth in revenues
3. Profit margin
4. Profit per employee

The results were analyzed using *stepwise regression* to demonstrate what factors move together (that is, are related) and *structural equation modeling,* predicting what causes what—in other words, *causation*—when there are multiple factors involved. Maister's statistical analysis was focused on defining what factors actually *caused* profitability. From this, Maister constructed the *Causal Model* of organizational financial performance (*see* Figure 3-1, page 30).

In its simplest form, the Causal Model statistically verifies the following predictors of financial performance:

1. Financial performance is **caused** by quality and client relationships.
2. Quality and client relationships are **caused** by employee satisfaction.
3. Employee satisfaction is **caused** by high standards, coaching, and empowerment.
4. High standards are **caused** by fair compensation, commitment, enthusiasm, and respect.
5. Coaching is **caused** by long-term orientation, commitment, enthusiasm, and respect.

The nine variables in this model (each box in the diagram) reflect more than 50% of all variation in profit performance of an organization. These results apply across

Figure 3-1. The Causal Model

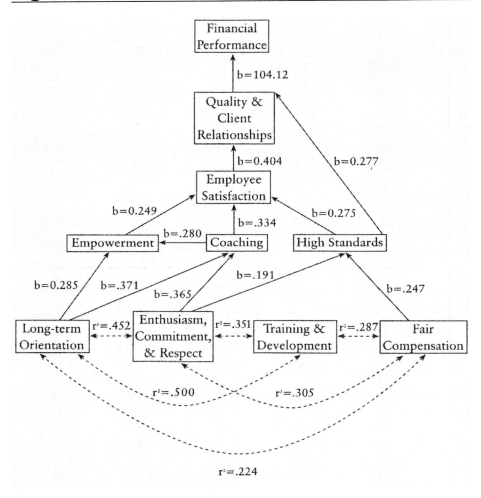

Source: Maister, D.: *Practice What You Preach: What Managers Must Do to Create a High Achievement Culture.* New York: Free Press, 2001. Reprinted with permission of the author.

all industries and cultures studied. Adapting these statistically confirmed conclusions to health care gives us the following extrapolations:

1. Financial performance is **caused** by quality service, care, honesty, empathy, and patient relationships (that is, relationship-based civil leadership).
2. Quality service, care, and patient relationships are **caused** by health care employee/provider satisfaction.
3. Employee/provider satisfaction is **caused** by high standards, coaching, and empowerment of their employees.
4. High standards of providers are **caused** by fair compensation, commitment, enthusiasm, and respect of fellow providers and employees.
5. Provider coaching is **caused** by long-term orientation, commitment, enthusiasm, and respect.

These five causal relationships are the very embodiment of civility-driven, relationship-based health care.

Maister's model *statistically proves* that a single-point improvement in the measure "Client satisfaction is a top priority at our firm" (on a six-point scale) results in a 104% increase in profitability! For illustration, imagine that an organization scores 3 out of 6 on a patient satisfaction survey in Year 1. In Year 2 it makes improvements that result in a score of 4 out of 6. The organization would realize a 104% *increase* in profitability during this time.

If this were a study confirming a new miracle oral medication that permanently cured diabetes, all providers would change their practice patterns today, based on the strength of the data. Why can't we in health care change our organizations based on this incredible data set? Why don't we start today? Relationship-based care is *the* key, and the basis of relationship-based care is civil leadership. To establish effective teams that focus on relationship-based care, an organization must establish a culture of civil leadership.

Health care is an industry dependent on effective relationships. Civility, including effective communication and interpersonal skills, is imperative and forms the base of Maister's Causal Model pyramid, leading to profitability. If providers and their organizations focus on high-quality care (the service component), client relationships (that is, relationships with patients), and employee satisfaction, all driven by the provider's civil leadership, profitability will increase. Simply put, when an organization energizes around doing the right thing, back-end profitability takes care of itself.

The DEPO Principle® Grows Up: The PPO Principle

In the interdependent reality of organizations today, leaders help set the strategy, and initiate and actively catalyze execution of the strategy through other stakeholders within the organization. They set the tone of the organization's culture by the way they communicate and behave, and through their focus. Creating a civil organizational culture is accomplished via the leader's open, effective communication, modeling of appropriate behaviors, and ultimately "walking the talk" for all within the organization (and beyond) to witness—in other words, acting with civility.

For an organization to perform well, leaders must maintain high-quality relationships with three groups: employees, customers, and investors. There is an interdependent value flow, beginning with the leaders, who affect the value employees perceive in their job, who in turn affect the value the customers perceive. The value that customers believe they have obtained translates into value for the organization, which means value for the investors.[22]

I have adapted this value chain to medicine and labeled it The DEPO Principle® (*see* Figure 3-2, page 33).

I developed this model about 10 years ago, but today's reality is that providers other than physicians are increasingly important in the direct delivery of care. Further, relationships between all the players are critical to optimal system function, maximal safety, and high quality. This trend is accelerating. Because of this, I have intentionally used the word *provider* in this book, intending to be inclusive of physicians, nurses, physician assistants, nurse clinicians, pharmacists, dietitians, and others. The DEPO Principle can, then, be revised to The PPO Principle (*see* Figure 3-3, page 33).

As you can see, the "DE" part of The DEPO Principle (Doctor → Employee) is nested within the Provider group of The PPO Principle. Further, the PPO emphasizes that health care is increasingly being delivered by capable nonphysician providers who must also step up to the civil leadership plate and ensure that effective relationship-based care is delivered.

Figure 3-2. The DEPO Principle®

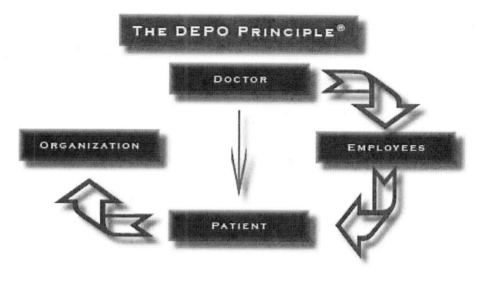

Source: © 2010 Michael S. Woods, M.D., M.M.M.

Figure 3-3. The PPO Principle

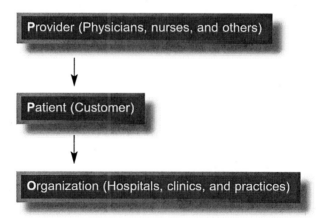

Source: © 2010 Michael S. Woods, M.D., M.M.M.

Relationship-Based Civil Leadership's Value in Medicine

Providers are the on-the-ground leaders in medicine. Every provider is the CEO of his or her practice, even if part of a larger group. Providers are responsible, of course, for results obtained and value perceived by patients. To ensure optimal patient satisfaction, it is crucial that a provider—as a leader in the interdependent reality of modern relationship- and team-based health care—ensure a satisfied, motivated office and hospital staff from the time patients are admitted to the hospital or greeted at the office door to the time they walk out the door at the completion of the visit. Providers, as leaders of medical organizations—regardless of their size—are, therefore, not only responsible for patient results, but also for the results obtained and value perceived by fellow health care employees—whether nurses, aides, housekeeping staff, receptionists, or floor administrators and assistants. This is true whether or not the provider is their direct employer (for example, organizational office or hospital-based employees). The relationship drives performance, whether that performance is measured in terms of safety, quality outcome, or dollars.

Interestingly, the reader will note that the seven items that form the base of Maister's pyramid of casual effect are aspects critical to relationship-based civil leadership and support the concepts of The PPO Principle. The provider can—and should—be accountable to self and the organization on these items—high standards, coaching, enthusiasm, and respect—as well as the others. Providers must be good stewards of their organization, to conserve fellow employees, promote quality and client relationships, and, ultimately, ensure the organization's financial health. The oft-used and tiresome saying is true: No margin, no mission. Relationship-based civil leadership promotes both margin and mission.

Four-Dimensional Provider Leadership

Providers are in unique roles as on-the-ground leaders. As described earlier, leaders are responsible for obtaining results with employees and for the results the employees obtain with the customers. However, individuals in leadership roles in other industries almost never have direct contact with the end customer, as providers do in medicine. For example, I own several computers, but Steve Jobs has never sold, delivered, or fixed any of the items I have purchased from Apple Computer (nor, for that matter, have any of his vice presidents or regional managers). I have interfaced only with the salespeople in the stores. Steve Jobs unquestionably affects Apple employees, and they affect me, as shown in the 3-D Model in Figure 3-4, page 35.

Figure 3-4. 3-D Model

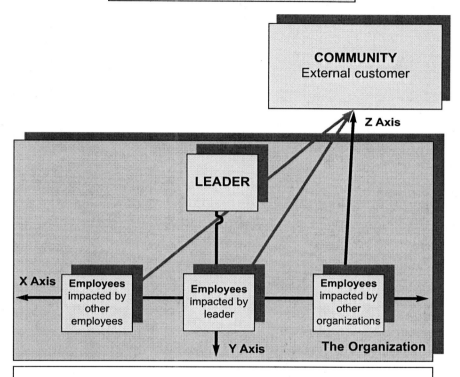

Y axis: *down* through the organization from the leader(s)
X axis: *across* groups and departments within the organization from internal employees impacted by the leader(s)
Z axis: *out* of the organization to the community or external customer, driven by employees impacted by the leader(s) internally

Source: © 2010 Michael S. Woods, M.D., M.M.M.

In other words, even though I am on the consumer "axis" and am outside the Apple organization, the leader still affects how I perceive value in what I am receiving, through the employees. This is the 3-D impact of the organization's leader.

In medicine, providers have a four-dimensional (4-D) impact (*see* Figure 3-5, page 37). Providers are unique as leaders because they not only have responsibility for ensuring that health care employees effectively interface and provide value to the end customer (patients), they also directly interface with the end customer and *directly deliver* added value.

To stick with the Apple analogy, the floor salespeople in health care are the nurses, receptionists, techs, administrative assistants, and so forth. Providers are in a unique leadership role, as they usually do not have responsibility in hiring, firing, or paying the people they lead in hospitals and other care environments, yet they determine, to a great extent, the level of satisfaction and effectiveness employees achieve. One "bad apple" (that is, unprofessional) provider can wreak havoc in an organization, creating turmoil and employee turnover that cost the organization hundreds of thousands of dollars per year, not to mention the increased malpractice risk and reduced safety and quality due to bad behavior or poor communication—incivility. The interaction patients have with the office or hospital staff is important in setting the tone for the entire patient visit, as the employees reflect the overall organizational climate. The need for a highly effective provider–employee relationship is clear.

Of course, providers interact directly with the end customer—the patient—too. If the patient's encounter—at any time from the initial telephone call to make the appointment until the time of leaving the office or hospital—with either the office/hospital staff or physician, does not meet the patient's expectations or is disappointing in some way, patient satisfaction decreases, and the potential for an unhappy, dissatisfied patient is increased.

The provider is the linchpin of relationship-based care, because he or she is the only individual who interacts with all other players. The provider has a more complex leadership relationship with the end customer than virtually any other business. Trust is a critical component of the provider–patient relationship, and the strongest predictor of trust is the physicians' communication style and interpersonal skills.[11,23–26] While there is much emphasis on patient satisfaction in health care

Figure 3-5. 4-D Model

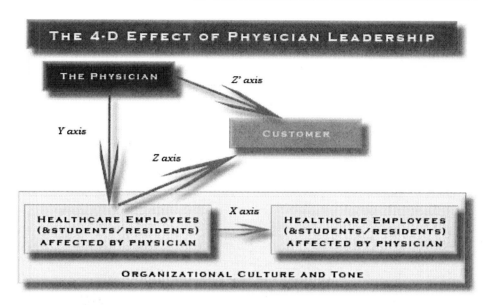

Source: © 2010 Michael S. Woods, M.D., M.M.M.

organizations today, the primary driver of patient satisfaction is, in fact, trust.[9] Trust is established between individuals—the provider and the patient—and it is only possible through effective communication and relationship building, driven by civil, relationship-based care.

The importance of provider communication as the basis for trust cannot be overestimated as the key to high-quality health care, improved outcomes, and lower liability. Trust in physicians has positive correlations to the following[8–11]:

- Adherence to treatment recommendations (that is, patient treatment compliance) and, therefore, outcomes
- Not changing physicians (that is, reducing patient loss from a practice and improving continuity)
- Not seeking second opinions, reducing overall health care costs
- Fewer disputes with the physicians (that is, less conflict, often the driver of complaints and malpractice and disability claims)
- The patient's perception of effective care and self-reported health

Hall has concluded, "Trust appears to be good for business, good for effective care, and good for reducing disputes."[27(p. 629)] Gosh, what a concept! And a key to developing trust, not just with patients but between all individuals working to provide care, is civility-driven, relationship-based care.

The provider–patient relationship, therefore, requires focus on the technical skills of effective personal leadership, communication, and interpersonal skills for the on-the-ground provider to optimally manage across all four dimensions in health care . . . and maximize profitability.

Few could credibly argue that enhanced civility, including professionalism, communication, and interpersonal skills, would not benefit the provider–patient relationship; what might be less apparent is the beneficial effect it would have between health care providers. It has been shown that nurses are particularly interested in having more interaction with physicians and often express the need to be listened to or respected more by physicians.[28] Such health care employee issues can be addressed by personal development related to areas of developmental need, ultimately enhancing the provider–employee relationship and benefiting the organizational or office culture. In the example of the nurses' desire for better communication and to be listened to or respected more by the physicians, coaching a provider to consistently demonstrate respect for individuals, to be a team player, and to help develop others would help resolve these concerns. How? By addressing—with the providers—the importance of demonstrating respect for the individual, which would benefit not just the nursing staff but all individuals the providers interact with. Emphasizing the interdependent reality of medicine would help the physicians to see nurses as fellow team members, not as subordinates and mere tools of patient care. Finally, putting the physicians into a teaching role and helping them to see themselves as developing others on the patient care team would enhance communication with the staff, as well as patient care. In short, the physicians benefit, employees benefit, and patients benefit. The PPO Principle tells us this, as does Maister's Causal Model.

The PPO Principle in Action

A good friend of mine, Tom Aug, the president of Development Partners (www.mydevelopmentpartners.com), whose mission is to "enhance the health care experience for all," is a believer in The PPO Principle. He implemented a physician leadership program in the University of Cincinnati's emergency room department. When he started the program, physicians didn't know the names of staff they worked with every day. Fifty percent of the nursing staff were temporary traveling nurses, reflecting a huge, constant turnover and a huge drain on capital resources. Departmental morale was so low you actually had to look up to see the bottom!

Within six months of the implementation of Tom's initiative, staff physicians knew the names of all the employees and started holding a dinner at a very nice restaurant once a month to get to know new staff members—regardless of whether the new employees were physicians, nurses, aides, or environmental services staff members. Imagine the effect this has had, especially on the nonphysician staff! They posted photos of every employee in the break room. The number of traveling nurses plummeted from 50% to 19%. My estimation of annual cost savings from this effort approaches a half million dollars! While patient satisfaction numbers are still pending, we know with certainty that where there are satisfied employees, there are satisfied customers. And this applies to medicine as well as to other fields. You can bet that patients are happier, too. This will translate (and is translating!) into greater organizational profitability, and you can be sure of enhanced quality and safety and lower malpractice claims risk, both individually and organizationally. This is a clear demonstration of the positive power of The PPO Principle.

Tom and I consulted briefly with a university medical center that illustrates The PPO Principle, albeit with the opposite outcome, illustrating that provider behavior is perfectly predictive of organizational tone. The challenges this university faced were (and I'm sure continue to be) massive in scope. Nursing staff told Tom and me about physicians doing procedures on intensive care unit (ICU) patients without sedation or anesthesia. Residents were openly rude and condescending to nurses because they saw attending staff treat nurses poorly, without any respect or politeness—and without any repercussions. No one was being held accountable for their actions or behaviors, which communicated to the young people in training that the organization did not enforce even minimal standards for behavior. In one of the ICUs where inappropriate behavior by providers (that is, physicians) had occurred, I asked the director, "Who is accountable?" His response summed up the entire day: "I don't know." In other words, as in many, many other organizations, standards of behavior existed, but no one knew who was empowered to enforce them, and they were ignored. This is the same as having no standards at all.

At this university, communication was, at best, unidirectional: downward. There was no mutual respect, no collaboration, no meaningful discussion or exchange of ideas, thereby stifling all creativity, all innovation, and all considered risk-taking to improve the environment. Nursing *openly admitted* to us that they would *intentionally not call* a resident or physician with potentially important information in order to avoid verbal abuse. In such a low-trust, abusive environment, civility-driven, relationship-based care—which requires open, multidirectional, cross-functional, interdisciplinary communication and mutual respect—is a fantasy. It has dramatic and very real *negative* effects on employee morale, patient satisfaction, and, worst of all, patient safety and outcomes . . . all witnessed in this organization. And who is, after all, responsible as the patient care team leader? The provider—usually a physician. That's The PPO Principle, again, albeit demonstrating ineffective leadership by physicians and senior administration—the CEO. What is worse is that it was a major teaching organization, where behavior was being propagated from attending to resident to medical student. Is it any wonder we all have a colleague or two who immediately comes to mind as we read this?

My message to the providers, the administration, and the legal department of this university, after listening all day to problem after problem, was what my message always is: There needs to be a focus on provider personal development, civil leadership, communication effectiveness, and accountability—and it needs to have teeth!

In short, there is no end to the degree of effectiveness an individual can achieve with other people, communication, or leadership. Everyone can improve his or her leadership and communication. And there is only one meaningful predictor of improvement: an individual's willingness to improve. Organizationwide initiatives can succeed, however, only with support from the CEO down and clear lines of accountability and expectations.

Physician Behavior and Malpractice

I have a wonderful video of my father's medical group of three, sitting around and discussing their 35 years of practice together in small-town Kansas. In that period of time, they never had a malpractice suit . . . in fact, they never even had a claim filed, surviving completely unscathed through two of the big malpractice crises in the 1970s and 1980s. I showed the video at a national meeting where the topic was apology and disclosure, or as I like to say, "apology and truth-telling." At one point in the video, one of my father's partners, Dennis Hardman, an internist, notes that he believed one of the reasons they were never sued was their "capacity to admit an error" and say "I'm sorry" when things went wrong. The video is a very powerful piece that emphasizes civil behavior, mutual respect, and kindness in relationships with partners and patients.

The speaker who followed me was a well-known figure from an Ivy League medical school, also speaking about malpractice, but from the perspective of the provider and the very significant negative effects a malpractice suit has on the provider's emotional health. She started her presentation by commenting on the video I had just shown. Her comments went something like this:

> *I really appreciated and enjoyed the video shown by Dr. Woods about the three old doctors in Kansas. But I would like to remind the audience that, like in the Wizard of Oz, "We're not in Kansas anymore." We aren't in Kansas, and the video is not anything close to the reality of today's world. It simply isn't like that for most of us.*

This speaker and I were on a panel after the morning session (and good-heartedly ribbed each other throughout the discussion), and we continued our conversation after the session, agreeing to go to dinner together and continue our chat. As so often occurs with me, I need time to digest conversations and don't like to admit I don't take perceived criticism well, yet I often simply "let things go," being inherently, and somewhat embarrassingly, conflict avoidant. As I pondered my friend's comments about the video, it occurred to me that she was both right and wrong. The reason she was right is obvious. The reason she was partly wrong was less obvious but nonetheless critically important: The video was not about malpractice in the 1990s. The video illustrated *a timeless way of being* . . . it was about 35 years of three physicians manifesting *effective, civil, civility-driven, relationship-based behavior.* You see, my friend did not initially understand that the results obtained by my father and his group had nothing to do with *when* (the 1960s to 1990s) or *where* (Kansas) they practiced. It was how they *were* around patients and colleagues that enabled and propagated their success. Their results would likely have been the same in Los Angeles or Boston. After I suggested this interpretation at dinner, my colleague felt differently about the video, too.

So if behavior is important in obtaining the results we desire, then enhancing providers' personal leadership, professionalism, communication, and interpersonal skills should result in lower malpractice liability. This is not mere conjecture. Consider these facts published in the medical literature:

- In 53% of cases, patients' decisions to call a malpractice attorney are due to poor relationships with providers before an injury.[29]
- The decision of a patient to litigate against a physician is often associated with a perceived lack of caring or availability, poor delivery of information, discounting of patient and/or family concerns, and failing to understand the patient's and/or family's perspective.[30]
- Physicians who have good communication and interpersonal skills have a lower liability risk. Physicians who have not been sued tended to spend more time per routine patient than those physicians who had been sued. Three minutes of additional time made this difference.[31]

A study published in *Journal of the American Medical Association* in 2002 provides undeniable proof that physician behavior is the driving factor in personal liability. Gerald Hickson, M.D., and his group at Vanderbilt University studied unsolicited patient complaints recorded by the medical center's patient affairs office.[32] The research hypothesis was "that unsolicited patient complaints will differentiate physicians at high and low risk of malpractice."[32(p. 2952)] The data reflect a medical staff of 645 general and specialist physicians over five years and three months. Forty-two percent of the medical staff had at least one risk management file based on an unsolicited patient complaint, and 22% were named in at least one lawsuit. Patient complaints were significantly associated with the opening of risk management files, risk expenditures, and lawsuits. The authors comment:

> *Results are consistent with previously published research on relationships between patients' dissatisfaction with care and malpractice claims. Patients who saw physicians with the highest numbers of lawsuits were more likely to complain that their physicians would not listen or return telephone calls, were rude, and did not show respect. Such complaints are similar to those documented in interviews with families who sued their physicians. In the present study, the total number of patient complaints, not any particular type, predicted risk management outcomes.*[32(p. 2955)]

An excellent summary statement of the actual cause of malpractice lawsuits also appears in this paper:

Risk seems not to be predicted by patient characteristics, illness complexity, or even physicians' technical skills. Instead, risk appears related to patients' dissatisfaction with their physicians' ability to establish rapport, provide access, administer care and treatment consistent with expectations, and communicate effectively.[32(p. 2951)]

The nail in the coffin regarding the effect of physician behavior and malpractice risk comes from Civility Mutual's research. Based on our own, long-held belief that physician personality (visible aspects of an individual's behavior) is a major driver of claims, we undertook a study to link physician personality to medical malpractice claims risk. Personality data were collected on more than 100 surgeons in a blinded study, using a validated personality assessment. The most recent five years of claims data were obtained for each participant, and regression and correlation methods were used to examine the relationship between claims and personality characteristics. The results revealed that personality characteristics were significantly predictive of claims in the past five years ($p < 0.01$) and were moderately but consistently correlated ($r = 0.31$ and $r = 0.34$ from pilot to validation sample, respectively).[33]

Even the risk industry is generating data that support communication failures as a major driver of litigation. In a conversation I had with Darrell Ranum, vice president of a medical malpractice insurance company in Ohio, he noted that a retrospective review of closed claims in their database found that fully 47% of claims could be traced back to some failure in communication on the part of the provider.[34]

Whether discussing organizational profitability or malpractice liability, one thing is clear: It all boils down to behavior. And civility-driven, relationship-based care is leadership.

Chapter Summary

- Uncivil behavior has profound effects on employee satisfaction, staff retention rates, health care outcomes, and an organization's bottom line.
- Relationship-based civil leadership provides the foundation for employee involvement and satisfaction, which translates to better patient safety and outcomes, according to David Maister's research.
- The PPO Principle (Provider → Patient → Organization) shows that the health care provider drives the health care quality process, with resulting benefits for patients and the organization as an entity.

- Providers have a four-dimensional impact on health care, affecting patient outcomes both through their work with fellow providers and with patients.
- It takes only one uncivil provider to create the possibility for a bad patient outcome.

References

1. Gonthier G., Morrissey K.: *Rude Awakenings: Overcoming the Civility Crisis in the Workplace.* Chicago: Dearborn Trade Publishing, 2002.
2. Rosenstein A.H., O'Daniel M. Disruptive behavior and clinical outcomes: Perceptions of nurses and physicians. *Am J Nurs* 105:54–64, Jan. 2005.
3. World H.: *The Violence That Ends Careers.* http://news.nurse.com/apps/pbcs.dll/article?AID=200661222029 (accessed Feb. 24, 2010).
4. Rosenstein A.H., O'Daniel M.: Impact and implications of disruptive behavior in the perioperative arena. *J Am Coll Surg* 203:96–105, Jul. 2006.
5. Sheth J.N., Sisodia R.S.: Marketing productivity: Issues and analysis. *Journal of Business Research* 55:349–362, May 2002.
6. Kaye B., Jordan-Evans S.: Retention: Tag, you're it! *Training & Development* pp. 29–34, Apr. 1, 2000.
7. Jones J.W., et al.: Stress and medical malpractice: Organizational risk assessment and intervention. *J Appl Psychol* 73:727–735, Nov. 1988.
8. Caterinicchio R.P.: Testing plausible path models of interpersonal trust in patient–physician treatment relationships. *Soc Sci Med Med Psychol Med Sociol* 13A:81–99, Jan. 1979.
9. Thom D.H., et al.: Further validation and reliability testing of the Trust in Physician Scale. The Stanford Trust Study Physicians. *Med Care* 37:510–517, May 1999.
10. Hall M.A., et al.: Measuring patients' trust in their primary care providers. *Med Care Res Rev* 59:293–318, Sep. 2002.
11. Safran G.D., et al.: Linking primary care performance to outcomes of care. *J Fam Pract* 47:213–220, Sep. 1998.
12. Leach M.J.: Rapport: A key to treatment success. *Complement Ther Clin Pract* 11:262–265, Nov. 2005.
13. The chief executive guide: The war for talent. *Chief Executive* Jul.–Aug. 1999.
14. Dean B.S., Krenzelok E.P.: The cost of employee turnover to a regional poison information center. *Vet Hum Toxicol* 36:60–61, Feb. 1994.
15. Buchbinder S.B., et al.: Estimates of costs of primary care physician turnover. *Am J Manag Care* 5:1431–1438, Nov. 1999.
16. Rosenstein A.H.: Nurse–physician relationships: Impact on nurse satisfaction and retention. *Am J Nurs* 102:26–34, Jun. 2002.
17. Kiel J.M.: Using data to reduce employee turnover. *Health Care Superv* 16:12–19, Jun. 1998.
18. Peltier J.W., Boyt T., Westfall J.: Using relationship marketing to develop and sustain nurse loyalty: A case of a rural health care institution. *J Health Hum Serv Adm* 22:83–104, Summer 1999.

19. Buerhaus P.I., Staiger D.O., Auerbach D.I.: Why are shortages of hospital RNs concentrated in specialty care units? *Nurs Econ* 18:111–116, May–Jun. 2000.

20. Tuna C.: Keeping workers earns a bonus in some offices. *The Wall Street Journal,* Jun. 30, 2008, p. B6.

21. Maister D.H.: *Practice What You Preach: What Managers Must Do to Create a High Achievement Culture.* New York: Free Press, 2001.

22. Personal communication between the author and David Ulrich, Jack Zenger, and Norm Smallwood about their book *Results-Based Leadership.*

23. Safran D.G., et al.: The Primary Care Assessment Survey: Tests of data quality and measurement performance. *Med Care* 36:728–739, May 1998.

24. Kao A.C., et al.: Patients' trust in their physicians: Effects of choice, continuity, and payment method. *J Gen Intern Med* 13:681–686, Oct. 1998.

25. Cook K.S. (ed.): *Trust in Society.* New York: Russell Sage, Foundation 2001.

26. Roberts C.A., Aruguete M.S.: Task and socioemotional behaviors of physicians: A test of reciprocity and social interaction theories in analogue physician–patient encounters. *Soc Sci Med* 50:309–315, Feb. 2000.

27. Hall M.A., et al.: Trust in physicians and medical institutions: What is it, can it be measured, and does it matter? *Milbank Q* 79:613–639, Dec. 2001.

28. Larson E., et al.: Hospitalk: An exploratory study to assess what is said and what is heard between physicians and nurses. *Clin Perform and Qual Health Care* 6:183–189, Oct.–Dec.1998.

29. Huycke L.I., Huycke M.M.: Characteristics of potential plaintiffs in malpractice litigation. *Ann Intern Med* 120:792–798, May 1994.

30. Beckman H.B., et al.: The doctor–patient relationship and malpractice. Lessons from plaintiff depositions. *Arch Intern Med* 154:1365–1370, Jun. 27, 1994.

31. Levinson W., et. al.: Physician–patient communication: The relationship with malpractice claims among primary care physicians and surgeons. *JAMA* 277:553–559, Feb. 19, 1997.

32. Hickson G.B., et al.: Patient complaints and malpractice risk. *JAMA* 287:2951–2957, Jun. 12, 2002.

33. Civility Mutual, Inc.: *Physician Risk Assessment Study* [data on file]. Civility Mutual, Inc., 1Q03, 2003.

34. Personal communication between the author and Darrell Ranum, Feb. 19, 2008.

Chapter Four

A Chasm of Disconnect: Community, Motivation, and the Patient

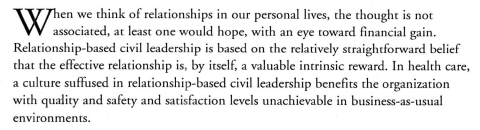

The engine for growth is patient perceptions. The engine for efficiency is process improvement.[1(p. 13)]
—Fred Lee

When we think of relationships in our personal lives, the thought is not associated, at least one would hope, with an eye toward financial gain. Relationship-based civil leadership is based on the relatively straightforward belief that the effective relationship is, by itself, a valuable intrinsic reward. In health care, a culture suffused in relationship-based civil leadership benefits the organization with quality and safety and satisfaction levels unachievable in business-as-usual environments.

A closer look at the evolution of the medical culture over the past 30 years and the extrinsic financial motivations of today that systematically replaced our forefathers' intrinsic motivations provides us with a contrast so bright that the need for relationship-based civil leadership as a critical focus in health care culture is undeniable.

While at first glance the content of this chapter may seem unrelated to the underlying themes of the book, I would suggest that this chapter highlights some critical barriers to gaining broad commitment to efforts at infusing relationship-based civil leadership in health care organizations today. I would suggest that the intent of health care providers in doing what they do is important to the topic of both relationships and civility.

Confusing Money and Motivation

As health care providers, what is our motivation? Is everything we do something that must be paid for? Is compensation the driver of our being? The concept of *nonmonetary value* is something many in health care have never learned—or perhaps, more accurately, we have un-learned it. Nonmonetary value is something or some activity for which one derives some form of gratification that is not based on the amount of money it either generates for the individual or requires an individual to pay.

My thoughts on this topic emanate from the brilliance of Dee Hock. I wish I had even a reflected twinkle of the amount of brilliance this man has, but in the absence of my ability to be original along these lines, I am going to rely on Mr. Hock. In his book *Birth of the Chaordic Age*, he writes a great deal about value and community:

> *One concept . . . I have puzzled over is an ancient, fundamental idea, the idea of community. The essence of community, its very heart and soul, is the nonmonetary exchange of value; things we do and share because we care for others, and for the good of the place. Community is composed of that which we don't attempt to measure, for which we keep no record and ask no recompense. Most are things we cannot measure no matter how hard we try. Since they can't be measured, they can't be denominated in dollars, or barrels of oil, or bushels of corn—such things as respect, tolerance, love, trust, beauty—the supply of which is unbounded and unlimited. The nonmonetary exchange of value does not arise solely from altruistic motives. It arises from deep, intuitive, often subconscious understanding that* self-interest is inseparably connected with community interest *[emphasis added]; that individual good is inseparable from the good of the whole; that in some way, often beyond our understanding, all things are, at one and the same time, independent, interdependent, and intradependent—that the singular "one" is simultaneously the plural "one."* [2(p. 42)]

Our society has become extremely skilled at monetizing everything. We hear statements suggesting this truism every day: "For enough money, you can have anything." "People will do anything if they are rewarded appropriately." "I'm not paid enough to do that." I could go on, but the reader has probably already generated several more of these examples. Think about how we speak about time: We earn it, spend it, and save it! "Time is money."

Hock continues:

> *Community is not about profit. It is about benefit. We confuse them at our peril. When we attempt to monetize all value, we methodically disconnect people and destroy community.*

> *The nonmonetary exchange of value is the most effective, constructive system ever devised. Evolution and nature have been perfecting it for thousands of millennia.*

It requires no currency, contracts, government, laws, courts, police, economists, lawyers, accountants. It does not require anointed or certified experts at all. It requires only ordinary, caring people.[2(p. 43)]

What health care provider—whether physician, nurse, or technician—and what health care consumer does not immediately understand the relevance to Hock's insight as it relates to medicine? There is perhaps no profession where "the monetization of value" has been more misguided and abused than medicine. We—*medicine and society*—have put virtually an infinite number of price tags on life and health. I, as a health care consumer, value my health so highly that I will, in fact, pay large portions of my income to maintain it or correct problems that arise. The question is "Should I have to?" A weightier question is, however, for me as a health care provider "Is this the way it *should* be?" Should everything I do—every bandage I change, every conversation I have with a patient, every waking moment I spend at work—be something that I *must* be paid for? Everything that used to fall under the concept of *caring* now has a DRG, CPT, or ICD code so we can submit a bill.

In his book *Healing the Wounds,* David Hilfiker has an entire chapter titled "Money." The final paragraph of the chapter reads as follows:

Like the medieval monastic practitioners, many (I think even most) of us physicians entered medicine with the desire to serve our patients, to be altruistic healers sacrificing ourselves for their good. Clearly, even the servant should be paid for working, so there is nothing contradictory between some remuneration and our calling. Yet as the profession has become wealthier and wealthier, a contradiction has arisen. As we physicians accumulate wealth, as we earn more than we really need, we become entrepreneurs and can no longer hang on to our perception of ourselves as servants. Yet we are not willing to let it go, either, to embrace the Hippocratic ideal of self-interest. So money becomes for us the hub of a very serious contradiction. At some hardly conscious level, my income proved paradoxically to be little more than an additional drain on my energies [emphasis added].[3(p. 183)]

The concepts of *nonmonetary* and *monetary* lead me to a discussion of intrinsic versus extrinsic motivation as it relates to the practice of medicine. Let's define *intrinsic motivation* as an activity an individual does simply because he or she enjoys it or derives some level of personal gratification simply because he or she is able to do it . . . enjoyment of the work or an activity for its own sake. On the other hand, *extrinsic motivation* is essentially *induced* behavior: "If you do this, you'll get that." The idea of extrinsic motivation is that if a positive reward is given out for a task, it will lead one to continue wanting to do the task, to keep getting the reward. It is, in essence, a method of controlling behavior and is, in reality, *no different than the promise of punishment if one does not do something*.[4] In other words, the promise of a reward could be reworded to say, "If you *don't* do that, you *won't* get this," which is, in essence, a form a punishment. Think of pay-for-performance: Is this not the perfect example of extrinsic motivation?

In his book *Punished by Rewards,* Alfie Kohn systematically destroys the myth that awards (extrinsic motivation), whether financial in the sense of pay-for-performance, or gold stars for the good behavior of children, succeed at achieving their intended effect. In fact, the evidence overwhelmingly suggests that *rewards fail miserably in efforts to induce lasting change*.[4] Kohn cites multiple studies that support this conclusion[4]:

- Undergraduate students who were asked to perform certain tasks without compensation performed the tasks significantly better than those who received compensation.
- The performance of college students who were paid for turning out school newspaper headlines stopped improving, while those who were not paid continued to get better.
- Fourth graders who were asked to perform a task they "liked" performed poorly at the same task when offered toys or candy as a reward for doing the task.

Kohn cites many other studies. Rewards—extrinsic motivations—significantly affect not only the *quantity* of one's work but also the *quality* of the work. While the provider may be thinking, "Well, medicine is different," the data do not support that conclusion. In fact, mere observation reveals to me—and probably to most of us—*that the effects of rewards in medicine are no different than in any other profession.*

Intrinsic motivation, conversely, is a powerful predictor of work quality and success. Koestner and colleagues have noted:

> *Intrinsically motivated people function in performance settings much the same way as those high in achievement motivation do: They pursue optimal challenges, display greater innovativeness, and tend to perform better under challenging conditions.*[5(p. 589)]

In simple language, "extrinsic motivators are a poor substitute for genuine interest in what one is doing." But Kohn points out an even more frightening fact:

> *What is likely to be far more surprising and disturbing is the further point that rewards, like* punishments, actually undermine the intrinsic motivation that promotes optimal performance *[emphasis added]*.[4(p. 69)]

In other words, even when individuals enjoy a particular job and are intrinsically motivated, providing extrinsic rewards to those individuals to do the work results in *reduced motivation* to do the very work they were previously motivated to do and a *reduction in the quality* of the results obtained. Who reading this book has not experienced the phenomenon that, at sometime in our past, we used to do something that we enjoyed—until we started getting paid for it? When we started getting paid for engaging in the activity (after which point we would no longer consider doing it for "free"), our intrinsic motivation was gone, or at least substantially diminished. Think of the fact that, not too long ago, physicians took emergency room (ER) call because it was part of their duty as part of the medical staff and in service to the community. Now, in many places, physicians will take calls only if they are paid to do so, and some do not provide this service at all. Kohn uses an "old joke" to illustrate this very point:

> *It is the story of an elderly man who endured the insults of a crowd of ten-year-olds each day as they passed his house on their way home from school. One afternoon, after listening to another round of jeers about how stupid and ugly and bald he was, the man came up with a plan. He met the children on his lawn the following Monday and announced that anyone who came back the next day and yelled rude comments about him would receive a dollar. Amazed and excited, they showed up even earlier on Tuesday, hollering epithets for all they were worth. True to his word, the old man ambled out and paid everyone. "Do the same tomorrow," he told them, "and you'll get twenty-five cents for your trouble." The kids thought that was still pretty good and turned out again on Wednesday to taunt him. At the first catcall, he walked over with a roll of quarters and again paid off his hecklers. "From now on," he announced, "I can give you only a penny for doing this." The kids looked at each other in disbelief. "A penny?" they repeated scornfully. "Forget it!" And they never came back again.*[4(pp. 71–72)]

The basic premise of this story—the fact that the old man began to pay the children for something they had been doing *voluntarily*, something they thought was fun, *changed the manner in which they viewed the activity.* Suddenly, "they came to see themselves *as harassing him in order to get paid,*"[4(p. 72)] [emphasis added] not because they enjoyed the activity. The old man's goal and, in fact, the result, was to sap the kids' intrinsic motivation.

This premise is directly relevant to medicine today. It is my belief that almost everyone goes into medicine driven by a substantial degree of intrinsic motivation, whether it be scientific interest or interest in doing good for humanity or, as Dee Hock expresses, community. But in the process of accumulating more than $100,000 of educational debt getting a medical degree,[6] students and residents see the money that physicians make in the form of clothes, cars, houses, and other accoutrements of wealth, and they listen to physicians complain about the discrepancy between what they get and what they *really* deserve; *our profession goes a long way in sapping the intrinsic motivation of our medical school graduates and residents before they are even out of training.* They graduate with expectations of extrinsic rewards that can never be met and that are virtually without end. What was once an intrinsically motivated passion becomes a job that doesn't pay me what I am "really worth."

As I reflect on my own medical education and transition from medical school, to residency, to fellowship, and practice, I can't tell you when this conversion happened to me, but it surely did. I can also tell you I did not, and do not, feel very good about allowing myself to fall into that trap. And I can't abdicate the responsibility for having allowed this to happen. I can't blame it on Medicare, Blue Cross, the HMOs, society, or anyone else. It is my opinion that the loss of intrinsic motivation due to extrinsic rewards is the primary reason *we have a profession stuffed with successful individuals, who are not happy or fulfilled in what they do . . . their intrinsic motivation got sapped* in the process of becoming a physician. If physicians truly did what they did because they loved their profession, why would the average age of retirement from the profession have dropped from 67 to 61?[7] Considering that this is an average, it reflects many physicians are retiring at a very young age.

Chapter Summary
- Dee Hock writes that self-interest is inseparably connected with community interest, that community is not about profit but about benefit.
- Alfie Kohn's research indicates that awards or extrinsic motivation—whether financial or otherwise—fail at achieving the intended effect of inducing lasting change.

- It is the author's opinion that the loss of intrinsic motivation due to extrinsic rewards is the primary reason that physicians are successful individuals who are not happy or fulfilled in what they do.

References

1. Lee F.: *If Disney Ran Your Hospital: 9½ Things You Would Do Differently.* Bozeman, MT: Second River Healthcare Press, 2004.
2. Hock D.: *Birth of the Chaordic Age.* San Francisco: Berrett-Koehler, 1999.
3. Hilfiker D.: *Healing the Wounds: A Physician Looks at His Work.* New York: Pantheon Books, 1985.
4. Kohn A.: *Punished by Rewards: The Trouble with Gold Stars, Incentive Plans, A's, Praise, and Other Bribes.* New York: Houghton Mifflin, 1993.
5. Koestner R., Zuckerman M., Koestner J.: Praise, involvement and intrinsic motivation. *J Pers Soc Psychol* 53:383–390, Aug. 1987.
6. Association of American Medical Colleges (AAMC): *Medical School Graduation Questionnaire, All Schools Report.* Washington, DC: AAMC, 2000.
7. Thrall, T.H.: Doctor dearth. *Hosp Health Netw* 75:50–51,54,56, Mar. 2001.

Chapter Five
Why Civility-Driven, Relationship-Based Care Now

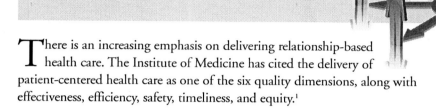

There is an increasing emphasis on delivering relationship-based health care. The Institute of Medicine has cited the delivery of patient-centered health care as one of the six quality dimensions, along with effectiveness, efficiency, safety, timeliness, and equity.[1]

Patient-centered medicine or health care has been defined as follows[2]:
1. Developing an understanding of the patient as a person
2. Conveying empathy
3. Finding common ground regarding treatment and goals of care

I have used this definition and the Institute of Medicine's desire for patient-centered health care as the guiding principles to assist providers with supplying civility-driven, relationship-based care and developing more effective communication and interpersonal skills. Interpersonal communication is the primary tool by which a provider and patient exchange information.[3] Effective interpersonal skills drive the personal relationship, the prerequisite for optimal medical care. Roter and Hall note that "talk is the main ingredient in medical care and . . . it is the fundamental instrument by which the doctor–patient relationship is crafted and by which therapeutic goals are achieved."[4(p. 3)] I am thrilled that any major health care organization is raising awareness of the patient-centered concepts. That acknowledged, I think we really need to talk about *relationship-based care.* The patient and provider aren't the only people involved in the care process. Many other individuals are involved, and I would suggest that the three-part definition above is required of any individual, as it relates to any other individual who is either providing or receiving care. Relationship-based care, then, is the goal, and it will result in quantum leaps in terms of patient safety, quality outcomes, and satisfaction across the health care spectrum.

Developing an Understanding of the Patient as a Person
A provider must understand his or her patient as a person and how various factors such as ethnicity, socioeconomics, and even gender can affect health care compliance

and outcomes. For example, there is no longer a debate about whether educating health care providers regarding multicultural issues is a good idea. Multicultural education of health care providers improves provider–patient communication, patient safety, outcomes, and patient and provider satisfaction. Further, interest in other cultures is one of the six Principles of Civility on which Civility Mutual bases its relationship-based civil leadership model (refer to Chapter 1).

The United States continues to be a popular immigration destination for non-English-speaking people from non-Western cultures. The nation is becoming more diverse, but access to and the quality of health care that individuals of immigrant groups will receive is determined by language and culture—and limited due to both the patient's and provider's expectations and experiences. To provide appropriate care for diverse populations and to help eliminate the health disparities that already exist, providers—any individuals caring for patients, whether physicians, nurses, allied health personnel, or pharmacists—must be equipped with increased awareness, knowledge, and skills in cultural competencies to better treat the increasingly diverse U.S. population. Such a focus requires providers to commit to learning *and leading* within their practice and organization.

Cultural competence—understanding the patient—is critical to the provision of quality care, and the perceived significance of cultural competence depends on one's role in the organization. Language remains a problem for patients and staff, although many hospitals have extensive translation services. Compared with management, staff and patients identify diversity as more of a problem.

Cultural sensitivity training has been documented to increase open-mindedness and cultural awareness, improve understanding of multiculturalism, and enhance ability to communicate with those from minority populations. Cultural sensitivity training programs improve knowledge and attitudes among health care providers and yield positive health outcomes for their patients.[5] Again, such training supports civility-based initiatives, and as providers gain such knowledge, tolerance and interest in other cultures, as well as respect and empathy, will improve.

Misunderstandings of important nuances between ethnic groups, especially based on stereotypes, can have a negative effect on health outcomes. Ethnic minorities have wide variations in health conditions and behaviors, and stereotyping can lead to spurious assumptions in caring for patients.[6] Stereotypes can be overcome only through education of health care providers. Ignorance is the greatest ally of stereotyping. In the civil leadership model, there is no role or reason for stereotyping.

Training programs in multiculturalism and culture can significantly improve an individual's understanding of the importance of assessing patient opinions and identifying important ethnic health beliefs, and they can positively affect a participant's attitudes about cultural competency issues.[7] These issues are critical to the civil leadership model and directly relevant to relationship-based health care, with direct implications for outcomes and safety.

My book *In A Blink* explores the depths of communication and how one can develop an awareness of patients' needs through assessment of six variables of communication—ethnicity, socioeconomics, literacy, gender, personality, and time. Remember that technical skill is one of the six Principles of Civility and that communication is a technical skill. Understanding these variables, which in turn helps a provider better understand the patient—enables one to adapt to the patient's communication needs.

Conveying Empathy (A Subsection of Relationship-Based Care)

Apology and truth-telling, as taught in my book *Healing Words,* as well as the communication techniques promoted and taught in *In A Blink,* are critical issues related to civility-driven, relationship-based health care. Barrier et al. note:

> *A physician-centered interview using a biomedical model can impede disclosure of problems and concerns. A patient-centered approach can facilitate patient disclosure of problems and enhance physician–patient communication. This, in turn, can improve health outcomes, patient compliance, and patient satisfaction and may decrease malpractice claims. Physicians can improve their communication skills through continuing education and practice.*[8(p. 211)]

Empathy, as you will recall, is one of the six Principles of Civility and a core concept in our civil leadership model.

Fortin notes:

> *While clinicians face increasing time pressure in caring for patients, communication*

with the patient can suffer. Communication is especially important in caring for the increasingly culturally diverse patient population in the United States. Different values, beliefs, and attitudes about health, illness, and health care can affect illness outcomes. These are best understood through dialogue. Patient-centered communication skills are associated with improved health outcomes, improved patient and clinician satisfaction, and less risk of malpractice suits.[9(p. 53–58)]

Cruz and Pincus, in a review of 25 articles in medicine and 34 articles in psychiatry, found the following:

Medical communication researchers have observed associations between physicians' communicative skills and patients' satisfaction, patients' adherence to treatment recommendations, treatment outputs, and patients' willingness to file malpractice claims. The research has also shown that primary care physicians can be more responsive to patients' concerns without lengthening visits.[10(p. 1253)]

Tangible Benefits of Civil Leadership and Relationship-Based Health Care

Risk Management

There is nearly universal agreement among risk managers in the United States, Canada, the United Kingdom, and Western Europe that anywhere from 47% to 80% of malpractice claims are attributed to failures in communication and/or a lack of interpersonal skills—usually of the physician. Reams of data support this statement. Hickson and colleagues concluded that physicians with the highest risk for lawsuits were poor listeners, often failed to return phone calls, and were rude and disrespectful to patients—all communication behaviors and all representing uncivil treatment of individuals.[11] Other research has found a statistically significantly higher risk of claims in surgeons who tended to be conflict avoidant and had poor team leadership skills, both indicative of less effective communication skills.[12] This, as noted earlier, has been confirmed using personality assessment analyzed against individual claims history. The Joint Commission has noted, "Physicians are most often sued not for bad care but inept communication."[13]

These same "inept communication practices" cited by the Joint Commission result in the majority of patient safety issues, as mentioned in Chapter 2. The Joint

Commission has collected sentinel event statistics since 1995, and in 1996 those data identified communication as one of the top five issues contributing to the generation of medical errors.[14] In 2009 that trend still held fast, as more than 64% of the 2,090 adverse events reported to the Joint Commission between July 2006 and June 2009 identified communication as one of the root causes.[15] Table 5-1, page 60, shows the areas where poor communication is most often a root cause of sentinel events.

Providers and organizations should view enhancing communication effectiveness through education and training as *the* link to lower liability. Eastaugh states, "The most common cause of malpractice suits is failed communication with the patients and their families. Explore ways that better communication could lead to fewer malpractice claims and allow health care organizations to reduce litigation costs."[16(p. 38)] Tongue et al. conclude, "Communication affects patient satisfaction, adherence to treatment, and physician satisfaction. Communication problems have also been cited as the most common factor in the initiation of malpractice suits."[17(p. 3)]

Stelfox et al. indicate, "A small number of physicians generate a disproportionate share of complaints from patients and of malpractice lawsuits. If these grievances relate to patients' dissatisfaction with care, it might be possible to use commonly distributed patient satisfaction surveys to identify physicians at high risk of complaints from patients and of malpractice lawsuits." Their study found, "Patient satisfaction survey ratings of inpatient physicians' performance are associated with complaints from patients and with risk management episodes."[18(p. 1126)]

Hickson et al., longtime researchers on the link between communication and liability, found in their seminal *Journal of the American Medical Association* article of 2002 that conflict avoidance—a communication behavior—resulted in more frequent unsolicited patient complaints.[11] They note, "Unsolicited patient complaints captured and recorded by a medical group are positively associated with physicians' risk management experiences."[11(p. 2951)] Educating and training providers in apology and truth-telling directly assists the provider in avoiding this pitfall, creating awareness and the skill set necessary to remain engaged after a bad or unexpected outcome.

Improved Quality of Outcome
Patient-centered practices, necessarily inclusive of civility-driven, relationship-based care, are related to a higher-than-average rate of compliance with treatment

Table 5-1. Top 10 Sentinel Event Types with Communication Identified as a Root Cause

Event Type	Percentage of Events with Communication Identified as a Root Cause
Elopement	88.8%
Delay in treatment	86.8%
Infant abduction	81.8%
Maternal death	81.3%
Perinatal death/injury	76.5%
Operative/postoperative complication	69.8%
Wrong-site surgery	67.4%
Medication error	66.9%
Restraint-related event	61.1%
Suicide	60.4%

Source: The Joint Commission Office of Quality Monitoring, Oakbrook Terrace, IL.

recommendations. Patient-centered communications and behaviors would therefore be expected to result in better patient outcomes.[19] Levinson has found that "Communication between a physician and his or her patient is a critical component of medical delivery" and that "The quality of communication affects patient satisfaction and health outcomes."[20(p. 226)] As noted earlier, effective communication leads to greater trust, which in turn results in better patient compliance, improving both patient safety and outcomes.

Reduction of Patient Safety Errors
Enhanced communication, of course, helps improve patient safety through improved clarity and understanding, which increases patient compliance with treatment and improves outcomes. Providers and their organizations are being directed to improve operational efficiency while simultaneously improving patient safety and health care quality. Unfortunately, providers have never received the education and training required to lead such initiatives, so they are struggling with

the process. Targeted training can reinforce the importance of the relationship-based care and help providers develop such practices.*

Communication Is Learned

Communication is a learned technical skill and one of the technical skills most lacking in health care. To understand that communication is learned, a simple illustration can help. We all either have children or know a child. Think about that child. Does that child speak? Assuming that there is no disability, of course! Where did the child learn to speak? Through observation of other people. Communication is *learned;* most communication skill is developed by observation and emulation. A commitment to improving our communication effectiveness can be made by enrolling in live or online e-learning courses, with a commitment to frequent, perhaps annual, refresher courses. There is evidence that online education can "produce *objectively* [emphasis added] measured changes in behavior as well as sustained gains in knowledge that are comparable or superior to those realized from live activities."[21(p. 1043)] Further, online material eliminates much of the time, cost, and travel requirements for education and allows constant, ongoing access for review of the materials and techniques so a provider can solidify the patient-centered communication practices.

In brief, the only reason one cannot improve his or her communication skills is not wanting to. From the standpoint of patient safety, quality outcomes, and medical malpractice liability, a conscious choice to improve communication sends a powerful message to our colleagues and patients. Not choosing to improve this facet of our technical skills also sends a message: that we aren't committed to maximizing our patients' safety and outcomes.

Chapter Summary

- Patient-centered medicine or health care includes understanding the patient as a person, conveying empathy, and agreeing on treatment and goals of care.
- Relationship-based care assumes that the patient, provider, and many others are involved in the patient care process, which requires communication and cooperation across a broad continuum of care and translates to increased patient safety, quality outcomes, and satisfaction across the health care spectrum.
- Studies have shown that communication failures are consistently among the most common root causes of sentinel or adverse health care events.

---

* Commercially available educational programs can help provide providers with facts, research, and practical tools to effectively diagnose and solve operational challenges while maintaining a focus on patient safety and quality outcomes. *See* http://www.civilitymutual.com and http://www.performax3.com.

References

1. Reinertsen J.L., Schellekens W.: *10 Powerful Ideas for Improving Patient Care.* Chicago: Health Administration Press and Institute for Healthcare Improvement, 2005.
2. Swenson S.L., et al.: Patient-centered communication: Do patients really prefer it? *J Gen Intern Med* 19:1069–1079, Nov. 2004.
3. Street R.L., Jr.: Information-giving in medical consultations: The influence of patients' communicative styles and personal characteristics. *Soc Sci Med* 32(5):541–548, 1991.
4. Roter D.L., Hall J.A.: *Doctors Talking with Patients/Patients Talking with Doctors.* Westport, CT: Auburn House, 1992.
5. Majumdar B., et al.: Effects of cultural sensitivity training on health care provider attitudes and patient outcomes. *J Nurs Scholarsh* 36(2):161–166, 2004.
6. Siriwardena A.N.: Specific health issues in ethnic minority groups. *Clin Cornerstone* 6(1):34–42, 2004.
7. Crosson J.C., et al.: Evaluating the effect of cultural competency training on medical student attitudes. *Fam Med* 36:199–203, Mar. 2004.
8. Barrier P.A., Li J.T., Jensen N.M.: Two words to improve physician–patient communication: What else? *Mayo Clin Proc* 78:211–214, Feb. 2003.
9. Fortin A.H., VI: Communication skills to improve patient satisfaction and quality of care. *Ethn Dis* 12:S3-58–S3-61, Fall 2002.
10. Cruz M., Pincus H.A.: Research on the influence that communication in psychiatric encounters has on treatment. *Psychiatr Serv* 53:1253–1265, Oct. 2002.
11. Hickson G.B., et al.: Patient complaints and malpractice risk. *JAMA* 287:2951–2957, Jun. 12, 2002.
12. Civility Mutual, Inc.: *The Use of a Standardized Personality Assessment in Determining Near-Term Medical Malpractice Risk* [data on file]. Civility Mutual, Inc., 2010.
13. Joint Commission International: *Communication Expert Panel Syllabus.* Oak Brook, IL: Joint Commission International, Oct. 5, 2006.
14. The Joint Commission: *Sentinel Event Database.* http://www.jointcommission.org/NR/rdonlyres/FA465646-5F5F-4543-AC8F-E8AF6571E372/0/root_cause_se.jpg (accessed Mar. 19, 2007).
15. Personal communication between the author and The Joint Commission Office of Quality Monitoring, Sep. 24, 2009.
16. Eastaugh S.R.: Reducing litigation costs through better patient communication. *Physician Exec* 30:36–38, May–Jun. 2004.
17. Tongue J.R., Epps H.R., Forese L.L.: Communication skills. *Instr Course Lect* 54:3–9, 2005.
18. Stelfox H.T., et al.: The relation of patient satisfaction with complaints against physicians and malpractice lawsuits. *Am J Med* 118:1126–1133, Oct. 2005.
19. Stewart M.: What is a successful doctor–patient interview? A study of interactions and outcomes. *Soc Sci Med* 19(2):167–175, 1984.

20. Levinson W.: In context: Physician–patient communication and managed care. *J Med Pract Manage* 14:226–230, Mar.–Apr. 1999.
21. Fordis M., et al.: Comparison of the instructional efficacy of Internet-based CME with live interactive CME workshops: A randomized controlled trial. *JAMA* 294:1043–1051, Sep. 7, 2005.

Chapter Six

Self-Inflicted Wounds: The Seven Common Leadership Missteps® of Physicians

Face reality as it is, not as it was or as you wish it were.[1(p. 38)]
—Jack Welch

This chapter is largely unchanged from my first book on leadership in health care, *Applying Personal Leadership Principles to Healthcare: The DEPO Principle*. It is included here because the information remains accurate. The basic premise of this chapter is that young providers learn much of the ineffective behavior encountered in health care during training. Yes, *learn*. Communication is a learned technical skill. It is an unfortunate reality that communication isn't the only behavioral characteristic providers learn to emulate. They can also be taught that arrogance is okay, that mistakes are intolerable, that position is power, and that, tragically, there are often no consequences for disruptive, abusive, or otherwise uncivil behavior.

This is disastrously illustrated by events recently reported in the popular press regarding a surgeon who has been a very influential figure in the profession. Known as an "old style" character—a kind term to describe a man who at best had a great many difficulties in dealing with women subordinates and peers—he ascended nonetheless to chairmanships and directorships with major physician organizations. He led, he researched, he published, and he advanced—until allegations including gender discrimination and general disagreement with senior management led to his resignation as chief of surgery from a major hospital in the northeastern United States.

The saddest part of all of this is that this individual could have done so many positive things for medicine simply by providing relationship-based, civil leadership . . . leading by example. He has been opposed to the things that he should have been leading. For example, he was a very vocal detractor regarding residency work-hour limitations. I had medical school colleagues who were surgery residents under this physician, and they described him as . . . well, those kinds of words usually shouldn't be printed.

If the profession doesn't confront these issues of behavior of our colleagues head-on, with recognition and transparency, *seeing reality as it is,* as Jack Welch advises us, we will lose our professional souls through complicity.

The Seven Common Leadership Missteps® of Physicians explain, at least partially, the current leadership behaviors seen in medicine today. *Missteps* are defined as *inappropriate behaviors or attitudes developed, manifested, and maintained by physicians—consciously or unconsciously—due to their education and/or personal, professional, or societal expectations.* Some of these behaviors have developed in response to the public or the public's perception of physicians and medicine. The seven Missteps can make the development and maintenance of civil leadership qualities difficult, and in some cases they actually form barriers to civil leadership practices. Some of the Missteps are distinct, while others are clearly intertwined with one or more of the others. I have fallen victim to many of these Missteps, as well as enabled many of them in my own life, and I will bring my real-life examples and observations to as many of the Missteps as possible for illustration. Keep in mind that awareness of the Missteps is key to self-perspective and the continuous improvement and learning Drucker and Bennis prod us to seek. This is about commitment to improvement, not perfection.

When I started thinking about leadership in medicine, I asked myself a couple of questions: "Why do physicians, despite being successful people, seem to have suboptimal personal leadership and interpersonal skills?" and "Why are the Principles of Civility violated so often?" I sat down and wrote out a list of 20 behavioral/attitudinal faux pas that I had witnessed or personally experienced in my own training and career, and I explored each in detail (*see* Box 6-1, page 67).

From my original list of 20 missteps, common themes emerged, and I grouped the missteps into seven general categories. When one of the original 20 missteps is first introduced as a component of one of The Seven Common Leadership Missteps, it appears as a subheading in **bold** print.

It will be clear to the reader that the behaviors and attitudes one observes in daily life may not fall neatly into just one of these seven general categories. The Missteps aren't black and white. For example, arrogance falls simultaneously under Misstep 2, "failure to consistently demonstrate respect for individuals" and Misstep 3, "lack

Box 6-1. The 20 Original Missteps in Personal Leadership

1. "Win–lose" paradigm
2. "Win–lose" education—competition
3. "Perfectionist" mentality—setting unrealistic expectations
4. The media—"Best Doctors List" (rating of doctors and hospitals)
5. Inability to negotiate
6. "Challenge" syndrome
7. The physician hierarchy—the "frozen bureaucracy"
8. "Chairman's syndrome"—positional "leadership"
9. "Captive audience phenomenon"—the abuse of residents, medical students, and staff
10. "Quick-fix attitude"—the acute care paradigm
11. "Quick-fix attitude"—Time
12. Physician self-deception: "I have the most important job in the world syndrome" and the failure to understand interdependence in the larger world
13. "Physicians are autonomous"—a persistent fallacy
14. Inability to self-assess
15. Difficulty providing behavioral feedback to other physicians
16. Over-focus on technical or intellectual ability as a proxy for leadership
17. Information overload
18. Reluctance to trust (resulting in self-protecting, self-serving behavior)
19. Failure to appreciate the importance of interpersonal relationships
20. Skepticism of "softer sciences" that have contributed to current leadership concepts (for example, sociology, management science, organizational analysis)

Source: © 2010 Michael S. Woods, M.D., M.M.M.

of personal leadership." Lacking integrity—that is, saying one thing and acting in a contrary manner—reflects more than a lack of personal leadership.

One thing I feel the reader must understand is that one of the many behavioral challenges we encounter in our profession is the fact—yes, *fact*—that behaviors are learned. We learn good things from our mentors. And we learn some not-so-good things. Dr. William Norcross directs a program in anger management for physicians at the University of California, San Diego. He notes that the disruptive physicians he encounters tend to be in high-pressure fields, such as neurosurgery, orthopedics, and cardiology.[2] Dr. Norcross suggests that disruptive behavior is perpetuated by "the brutal training surgeons get, the long hours, being belittled and 'pimped.'"[2(p. D1)] The "whole structure teaches a disruptive behavior."[2(p. D1)] In other words, young physicians learn such behavior from staff attendings. And unfortunately, there are few examples of such staff physicians being held accountable for such actions, which sends the message that if you are important enough, you can get away with anything. Therefore, change, including holding individuals accountable for behavioral standards, must be from top to bottom . . . and especially at the top!

The Seven Common Leadership Missteps of Physicians

1. Failure to seek win–win solutions
2. Failure to consistently demonstrate respect for individuals
3. Lack of personal leadership
4. Lack of flexibility
5. Inability to be a team player
6. Failure to develop others
7. Lack of openness

We are all half-baked experiments—mistake-prone beings, born without an instruction book into a complex world. None of us are models of perfect behavior. We have all betrayed and been betrayed; we've been known to be egotistical, unreliable, lethargic, and stingy; and each one of us has, at times, awakened in the middle of the night worrying about everything from money, kids, or terrorism to wrinkled skin and receding hairlines. In other words, we're all bozos on the bus.[3(p. 28)]
—*Elizabeth Lesser*

Misstep 1: Failure to Seek Win–Win Solutions

"I know some people who think a win-win situation means 'We kick their butts twice!'"[4(p. 180)]
—*Gary Dehkes*

The most destructive things to the development of personal leadership skills in the medical profession begin and end with how we train physicians. In fact, many of the sections that follow can ultimately be linked back to our education as physicians. The educational process of a physician is a competitive game with fellow students and residents. And once a physician is in practice, competition continues with his or her own partners and other groups within a hospital or community—only now the competition is for patients, income, and prestige. Shell and Klasko note, "Many doctors can recall being warned during their first premed orientation session to: 'Look to your right and look to your left—only one of you will make it into medical school.'"[5(p. 4)]

Because of the way we are selected and educated, we end up seeing everything as "win–lose." We compete in college with our classmates to get into medical school. If you get in, you "win." Someone else loses, but you have gotten what you wanted. In medical school we compete for ranking in the class, in competition with all other medical students, so we can get the best residency. You win, and someone else— usually faceless to you—loses. In residency we compete for fellowship: win–lose. From fellowship we compete for the best jobs: win–lose. In practice we compete with other groups or physicians in the same city for patients and for health care contracts: win–lose. In practice, the win–lose thinking always . . . yes, *always* . . . devolves into competition for money, not patient care or quality outcomes. (The arguments are usually thinly veiled by attempts at linking the issue to safety and quality, but there is almost without failure an underlying economic concern.) And while you may be thinking, "I never thought about someone else being a loser," the reality is that the mind-set created by this training is very much "win–lose." "Win–lose" competitive selection and thinking do not promote respectfulness of the other individuals involved in the competition or of negotiation.

Without question, changing the educational system and eliminating this win–lose attitude would benefit all those involved in health care—provider, employee, and patient alike. It is impossible to lead if one thinks one must always win.

The Media—"Best Doctors List." The media contributes to the medical professions' dysfunctional win–lose attitude. The concept of ranking physicians and hospitals is, itself, rank. It is misguided and creates *an illusion of value.* Unfortunately, this is something that physicians and hospitals have taken up with gusto akin to that of a starving dog having just found a unemptied garbage can. Entire groups and hospitals now use such misleading rankings in advertisements for themselves.

U.S. News and World Report does one such ranking annually, in a feature titled "America's Best Hospitals." Although the publication has acknowledged in the past that "sophisticated" medical care is now widely available, its honored institutions "provide a degree of specialized care few community hospitals can match."[6(p. 44)] What the publication fails to note, however, is that its methodology is suspect, if not overtly flawed, and most people don't require "specialized care." *Ranking increases competition* between the ranked institutions, especially academic centers, which, in fact, are the bastions of win–lose thinking in medical education.

Health care's focus should be on creating win–win solutions—improving all of health care delivery in all geographic areas with the available funds, instead of worrying about "who is best." Ultimately, trying to define "who is best" is counterproductive, inducing even more unhealthy competition in medicine, and it is, in the end, meaningless. We need to ask ourselves, "Are we delivering the best-quality and safest care possible, *given our resources*?" We should not be asking whether a critical access hospital can deliver the same care as a university medical center.

The practice of ranking serves only two purposes: It gives institutions and physicians inappropriate and unhealthy advertising ammunition, and it stimulates unhealthy and expensive competition and service redundancy, potentially resulting in hospitals adding services simply in the interest of economics—to compete with the hospital down the street. *Both of these outcomes increase health care costs, probably without substantial benefit to patients.*

Leaders and institutions don't need to beat anybody. They just need to be the best they can be with the resource constraints of their specific situation.

Inability to Negotiate. Negotiation, to most physicians, simply means getting what they want . . . that is, again, winning. Basically, when I have seen physicians negotiate, the process often takes the form of overpowering the opposition through professorial proclamations of position or facts, with little appreciation or regard for the other party or their position, assuming that the other party is even *heard*. It is the simple abuse of positional power. While there are clearly some very skilled physician-negotiators, the profession generally has much to learn about the skills of listening and negotiating, as well as the concept of win–win.

Shell and Klasko outline some of the same principles outlined in my 20 original missteps in physician leadership. They describe "biases physicians bring to the table" of any negotiation process as barriers to physicians being effective negotiators. They list the following biases that physicians bring to the negotiation table[5]:
- The competitive us-versus-us bias
- The autonomy bias
- The hierarchy bias

The competitive us-versus-us bias is highlighted by an example of the difference between business school students and physicians, each given exactly the same negotiation problem to solve. The goal of the exercise is for each group to find the hidden solution, demonstrating the ability to find and exploit win–win interests. Coming up with the solution in the exercise actually *doubles* the amount of money both parties can make from the transaction. In this model, about 8 of 10 M.B.A. students or business executives will eventually find the win–win solution. When physicians are given this same problem, almost *none* of them are able to solve the problem. Shell and Klasko note:

> . . .*the physicians seem hesitant to risk cooperation, fearing a win/lose result that might make them look bad. Indeed, in debriefing the case,* doctors sometimes express the feeling that they would rather have everyone lose than give anyone else a chance to get more than his or her fair share *[emphasis added]. Finally, the worst solutions come from mixed groups of physicians, i.e., attendings, residents, and medical students. These groups find it almost impossible to cooperate.*[5(p. 4)]

The authors note, as has been done in this book, that medical education is responsible, at least in part, for this finding. Covey refers to this type of negotiation outcome as the *Scarcity Mentality*™, where people believe they need to get as much of a fixed pie as they can, to the exclusion of others, and before anyone else can get more than them.[7] The situation described above is, in fact, the ultimate illustration of the Scarcity Mentality described by Covey.

In order to lead, one must be able to and have the desire to find the win–win solution more often than not.

Misstep 2: Failure to Consistently Demonstrate Respect for Individuals

All day long I was being asked for advice. All day long I was considered indispensable. Even outside the office I was treated with deference. It was only too easy to perceive myself as inherently more important than others.[8(p. 154)]
—David Hilfiker, M.D.

Respect for individuals can be violated in many ways, some so subtle that we may not even appreciate these violations when we commit them. Of the original missteps identified, "the 'perfectionist' mentality," "physician self-deception," and "failure to appreciate the importance of interpersonal relationships" clearly relate to respecting people, respecting their thoughts, and acknowledging and being understanding of human fallibility. The concept of the "captive audience phenomenon" is also introduced in this Misstep. If one stops and ponders the material of this section as it relates to patients, much of what is really being discussed revolves, essentially, around the misguided and oft-abused—in fact, ridiculous—concept of "clinical detachment."

The Physician Hierarchy—The "Frozen Bureaucracy." Hierarchy can violate respect for the individual when it is used in a superior–subordinate fashion. It might be acceptable, albeit doubtfully, if the physician hierarchy ended within the profession itself. It could be argued that such a hierarchical arrangement is merely an unattractive aspect of the profession. But it is much more damaging than that, especially to our relationships with employees and patients.

The authority of physicians can clearly be an *inhibition* to optimal interpersonal relationships and respect for the individual, especially as it relates to communication. Just think about the data already presented about nurses not clarifying orders with physicians they are afraid of . . . or the resident who didn't call the attending because he was afraid . . . remember? The baby died.

A physician is given a tremendous amount of respect, and a great amount of credence is given to his or her opinions on matters not only of medicine but of all things. And often this "respect" is given without any question or without any previous demonstration that such "respect" is deserved. Observes Dr. Hilfiker:

> *As a new physician fresh from my internship, I was amazed at the considerable authority invested in me, not only in my consulting rooms but also among office and hospital staff and even within the general community.* My position as physician automatically conferred upon me an authority that was independent of my abilities. *[emphasis added]*[8 (p. 153)]

" . . . an authority that was independent of my abilities": What an incredible and awesome responsibility! What is a bit frightening about this statement is that many young physicians finishing training *expect* this sort of reception. And they, in fact, more often than not, receive it. This can certainly lead to a self-perpetuating hubris that few other professions can afford (or get away with).

This type of unearned respect, the near deification of the physician—whether just out of training, or in his or her 25th year of practice, is damaging to the patient, health care employees, and the physician. It can lead to the physician developing a damaging sense of indispensability and results in an interpersonal chasm between the physician and patient, inhibiting honest communication and therefore preventing—yes, preventing—the best outcomes.

Avoiding Misstep 2, "failure to consistently demonstrate respect for the individual," requires that one begin to relinquish this destructive, misplaced, and unearned authority—and comprehend how correct Hilfiker is in stating that such authority, and clinging to it, prevents us from having "healing relationships with [our] patients."[8(p. 153)] It requires giving up autonomy and becoming a team player.

Hierarchy also is one of the most potent equilibrium enforcers. The medical hierarchy is on a slow but accelerating downward spiral to death. The hierarchies in medicine, especially within universities, are often the drivers of "persistent social norms, corporate values, and orthodox beliefs about the business,"[9(p. 32)] as well as medical education. This type of equilibrium results in a failure to respect individuals who are trying to push the organization to the edge of chaos and drive beneficial change throughout the system. Hierarchies, as we know in medicine, are antithetical to the reality of the complex adaptive system that health care is.

The "Perfectionist Mentality." The "perfectionist mentality" is another concept pervasive in medical training. It is the idea that, as a physician, you should make error-free decisions—that mistakes are intolerable and unacceptable. And, frighteningly, there are some physicians who really believe this and think it is nothing short of blasphemy for me to suggest otherwise. Unfortunately, such an attitude creates unrealistic expectations that can be fulfilled by no one and creates guilt in all who make mistakes . . . everyone. It has been said, "Perfection is apparently not what life is about at all, since perfection is nonexistent. Since we are not perfect, we have to be accountable."[10(p.8)] Further, it prevents people from achieving their best, as in a no-mistakes environment, no matter how unrealistic, avoiding failure becomes more important than solving problems, and "that's a surefire way to avoid being successful."[11(p. 96)]

Hock probably summarized this concept best, even though he was speaking about society in general, when he said, "We need the legitimization of doubt." He paraphrased this by saying, "Admitting the possibility that we don't know all the answers is the difference between hubris and humility."[12] It is okay to not know the answer to everything—and, in fact, be willing to openly admit it. There is a humorous ridiculousness to the concept that physicians—or anyone else for that matter—should make error-free decisions when dealing with human beings. Think of it in this way: It has been estimated that there are 10^{300} possible moves in the game of chess.[13] This number of possibilities exceeds the number of milliseconds since the Big Bang that created our universe. It exceeds the number of elementary particles in the observable universe.[14] With this much possibility, with so many dynamic combinations in all systems—let alone the human, who has a thousand times as many genes as the chess game—doesn't it seem outrageous, in fact laughable, to think we should always know the answer? Doesn't it seem misguided to expect perfection in decisions about diagnosis and treatments in the face of essentially limitless diversity and potential for unpredictable biological response?

To get away from this perfectionist mentality is a step in the right direction of not only respecting individuals but also learning about compromise and listening to and respecting alternative points of view. In a way, it is like evolution—increasing the genetic diversity of medical thought—as opposed to the current tendency toward medical monoculture—or the "one right way, and it's my way" attitude.

The "Captive Audience Phenomenon." Medical training involves a win–lose series of educational steps, and it also occurs in one of the few professions where if you don't like the program you are in, you have two choices: suck it up and put up with it or quit. The likelihood of medical students or residents actually being able to transfer into another training program is essentially nil. Because medical students and residents have developed the win–lose mentality through the training they have endured, to quit is a double-whammy: Not only will they not get another chance, they lose. Because of this system, medical students and residents are, functionally, a captive audience, serving at the pleasure of the medical school and attending staff.

Physicians might want to consider the following question: Were you treated with the same degree of compassion and consideration during training that your attendings professed to have for their patients? Were you treated as well as your attendings treated their own family? What message do residents receive when they are verbally or mentally abused and in the next breath told to have compassion for patients? This reflects a disconnect between an attending's (or any other physician's) words and actions—in other words, it reflects *a lack of personal integrity.* It is an issue of personal respect for the individual.

"Induced behavior is the essence of leadership, no matter how modest. Compelled behavior is the essence of tyranny, no matter how benevolent,"[12] Hock says. Note that he does not mean inducing behavior through intentional instillation of guilt in people, as so often occurs in medical training.

An underlying premise of such a teaching approach is the misconception that one can't be compassionate and considerate of residents and medical students and still be demanding as to the quality of their performance. One can be both. That's what civility-driven, relationship-based care is all about!

Why don't we let residents transfer to other programs at will and force institutions to compete to keep the best people, as in other knowledge-based industries? This would actually provide incentive for staff to treat students and residents respectfully, and it would promote more humane design of training programs to retain residents. This sort of approach—competition for the best talent—has resulted in remarkable things in the high-tech industry; why wouldn't it work here?

Another group that is a captive audience, albeit not as fixed as residents or medical students, is physician office staff and hospital staff. Let's face it—physicians work with their staff virtually every day of their professional life. We see our staff more than we see our family in some cases. Consider the experience of a nurse practitioner I spoke to recently:

> *Nurse practitioners work in collaboration with physicians in varied roles throughout the health care system. Within the medical arena, patients consider [nurse practitioners] as physician colleagues and they are expected to function independently. However, in reality, we are still seen as merely "nurses" by physicians, in a subordinate role . . . not as a partner in patient care.*
>
> *My experience has been limited to primary care. Regardless of the experience—or inexperience—of the physician, doctors have always occupied the "lead provider" roles. A nurse practitioner in the "lead provider" role, defining the expected numbers and generated income for the doctors would be heresy, even though it is reality in many cases.*

This individual provides substantial support to the office she works in (both financially and personally), reduces the burden of the physicians she works with, and still feels like, and is treated as, a subordinate, an instrument by which care is delivered . . . not a partner. Again, a lack of respect for the individual and the value the individual brings to the practice is demonstrated.

The "captive audience phenomenon" isn't merely a concept. It's real. Physicians need to learn the concept espoused in nonmedical businesses that one should treat employees as the best customers or, in fact, volunteers. Physicians should learn to treat their staff, residents, and medical students as they do their most important patient. In the end, the concept of "you can buy their hands but not their hearts; you can buy their backs, but not their brains" should stimulate us to win the hearts *and* brains of medical students, residents, and staff. If we do that, their hands and backs will willingly follow. The statement that "people do not care how much you know until they know how much you care" is a truism.

Physician Self-Deception. The misstep "physician self-deception" plays into respect of the individual. Physicians are often taught that they have the most noble and important job in the world. To have an attitude that one's job is the most important is an extremely unbecoming attitude to have and can result in disrespect of others' work and occupations. It is a form of self-deception. We in medicine are just part of the social fabric and the overall economy. We have an important job, but we need to respect what others do as being just as important to society as what we do. It is an interdependent reality. If all physicians decided to strike, the effect on society would be minimal. Only the sick would particularly care; all others would simply be mad at us. Few individuals are going to have empathy for the strike of a profession where the average income puts most individuals in the 90th to 95th percentile of all workers in the world.

How many times have you seen a city brought to its knees because of a sanitation workers' strike? Many—recall New York City and Philadelphia. How many times have you seen a significant portion of the country paralyzed by an airline pilots' strike? Think of United Airlines in the summer of 2000. What about a teachers' strike? public transportation? How about Los Angeles, fall 2000, when more than 450,000 people couldn't go to work or buy groceries for a month because of such a strike. Quite frankly, a hospital nurses' strike would have a greater impact on society than would a physicians' strike, in my opinion. Who would take the orders? Who would empty the bedpans? (Probably the medical students and residents in training programs!) It would be akin to every soldier below the rank of general deciding not to go to the war. How effective would such an army be?

Many of the concepts related thus far, including self-deception, result in physicians having a divorce rate higher than those in many other professions. I have known physicians who justify their failing to carry out responsibilities as a spouse in the name of having responsibility to patients first. Even marital problems can start in or result from the educational process in medicine. I recall interviewing for a particular surgery residency where I was told, "If you are married when you come, you will leave single. We have a 100% divorce rate among our surgical residents." And worse, this was stated proudly, like it was a badge of worthiness and that the people accepted were so dedicated to medicine that they sacrificed all else just to come to the program. How sick is that? And what does it teach young people about the value of relationships?

Finally for this misstep, we return to the concept of efficiency and relationships with people—in this case, our patients. As Covey has stated, we are efficient with things and effective with people,[15] and physicians often forget this. This concept of efficiency in medicine is not novel. In Hilfiker's book *Healing the Wounds,* he succinctly captures problems related to failing to understand the difference and the result of *efficiency* in a doctor–patient relationship:

> *When the physician finds that he is not taking the needed time for reflective meditation upon the meaning of his job, when he finds he is using laboratory tests and x-ray studies instead of in-depth interviews, when he is giving pills instead of counseling or explanation, when he himself is not getting his needed sleep; at these points the physician needs to ask himself whether the values of efficiency and productivity have not in fact gained the upper hand, submerging other important medical and human values. Has productivity become a goal in itself? Has the attempt to meet more and more patient needs ultimately turned into its opposite? Has the physician become a servant, not of his patients, but of productivity and efficiency themselves?* [8(pp. 144–145)]

Efficiency, in this light, begins to lose its luster. We don't need more efficiency in medicine; we need more effectiveness. In fact, Hilfiker actually addresses this topic head-on elsewhere in his book:

> *The unintended consequence is that the person tends to disappear and the patient becomes an object, a thing upon which the physician acts. It is no accident that the talk of medical personnel is filled with references to people as if they were diseases or parts of the body. "Dr. Hilfiker, there's a broken leg in the ER" may sound humorous out of context, but it reflects the reality of medical detachment.* [8(p. 127)]

In civil leadership, one respects all individuals at all times and in all situations, regardless of status and title. Civil leaders treat people by the same principles, whether they are a patients, family members, residents, or nurses.

Misstep 3: Lack of Personal Leadership

Most powerful is he who has himself in his power.
—Lucius Annaeus Seneca

This Misstep might be a super-category that incorporates the other six. So many things affect the ability of one to lead, but as Hock notes, it basically comes down to spending a lot of time working on oneself.[12]

This Misstep is composed of at least 3 of the original 20 missteps: "chairman's syndrome," "captive audience syndrome," and "over-focus on technical or intellectual ability as a proxy for leadership." And, of course, "physician self-deception" heavily influences this Misstep.

The "Chairman's Syndrome." Harry Fritts Jr., notes that "the attitude a chair should try to cultivate may charitably be called self-delusion or, uncharitably, arrogance."[16(p. 78)] Jim Collins writes, in *Leading Beyond the Walls*, that "executives must accept the fact that the exercise of true leadership is inversely proportional to the exercise of power."[17(p. 25)] He goes on to explain that many business executives confuse leadership with power, and that older executives complain of the lack of loyalty in the younger generation. However, he points out that there is no less loyalty in the younger generation. They are simply less willing to grant power to a single organization or person, are less subservient, and ultimately have more freedom. He concludes, "the most productive relationships are in their essence mutual partnerships rooted in a freedom of choice vested in both parties to participate only in that which is mutually beneficial and uplifting."[17(p. 28)] This looks exactly like heath care today. Many times I have heard attending physicians and partners say, "All these younger people are interested in is work–life balance." This is simply not true. They are just less willing to sacrifice for the sake of sacrifice.

In the preceding paragraph, if one substituted the word *chair* or *attending physician* for *older executive* and substituted *medical student, resident, fellow,* or *office staff* for *younger generation,* it would look pretty similar to medical education today. The major difference is that med students, residents, and fellows don't have the flexible options that those in the business world have, as they are essentially a captive audience, a concept introduced earlier.

We have discussed the win–lose aspects of medical training. Now we are concerned with the pecking order that is so often reinforced—consciously or not—in medical training. Again, I quote Shell and Klasko:

More than most professions, a medical title carries expectations as to how those above and below that status will be treated. Age, merit, and value often take a back seat to professional status and academic rank. In an almost militaristic order, medical faculty line up in front, while attendings, residents, interns, students, nurses, and other staff fall into place behind them.[5(p. 5)]

Unfortunately, this truth can carry over to patient care, as it relates to an individual's opinion about a treatment or an intervention. I have seen, as we all have, a medical student or resident make a suggestion about the treatment of a patient that is better than the regimen planned by a more superior individual (in the hierarchical sense), only to be squelched by that person in order to keep the superior–subordinate roles intact; in the private recesses of their intellect, it is hoped that they recognized the value of the medical student's recommendation. I know I was guilty of this on more than one occasion. The "chairman's syndrome" is really about the concept of *positional or borrowed leadership*—that is, an attitude that, because of one's position, one should automatically be deferred to and that this translates into leadership. Margaret Thatcher, the former prime minister of Great Britain, has been quoted as saying, "Being in power is like being a lady. If you have to tell someone you are, you aren't."

In general, individuals who practice such forms of leadership usually create low-trust environments and really aren't in power; they just control. It is, in fact, a failure of personal leadership and lack of understanding of the importance of interpersonal relationships, all rolled up together. And as they say, if you think you are leading but no one is behind you, you are just going for a walk. When such practices dominate the environment from the chair on down, it is destructive, and it is neither useful nor helpful in building working relationships between peers, residents, or students. Further, because the teaching staff is the model for the trainees, *the behavior is learned and perpetuated by those in training*. Residents treat medical students in this fashion when that is all they have seen in their own training program. Remember the story at the beginning of the chapter? What was that physician leader's behavior teaching the residents and medical students at one of the most prestigious schools in the country?

Lest some physicians dismiss this concept of "captive audience" and "physician hierarchy" as hogwash, let's look at some exceedingly powerful data from medical students providing input into the *2008 GQ Program Evaluation Survey, All Schools*

Summary Report from the Association of American Medical Colleges (AAMC).[18] I have included, for an interesting perspective, the results from both 2008 and 2004:

- In 2008, 84.4% of medical students reported being *publicly belittled* or *humiliated* at least once. In 2004, 83.1% reported this abuse.
- 55.5% of medical students reported being *publicly belittled* or *humiliated occasionally or frequently* in 2008, compared to 57.6% in 2004.
- In 2008, 22.9% of medical students reported being subjected to offensive sexist remarks/names at least once, and 13.2% occasionally or more often. In 2004, 26.4% of medical students reported being subjected to offensive sexist remarks/names at least once, and 16.9% occasionally or more often.
- In 2008, 25.5% of medical students reported being required to perform personal services (for example, shopping, babysitting) at least once, and 12.9% occasionally or more often. This compares to 23.4% and 13.5%, respectively, in 2004.

Several things must surely strike the reader as, well, embarrassing for our training programs. The most obvious is that there seems to be very little progress being made with regard to inappropriate behavior of residents and staff. And who is ultimately responsible for these results? The leaders in medicine. Who is responsible for delivering the results? Those who act with incivility.

Second, one may quibble, saying, "What do they mean by 'humiliated'?" If being required to perform personal services does not imply a *captive audience*—that is, individuals afraid to *not* comply with a superior's request for personal services— what else are these data telling us? Any one of the bullet points above should embarrass our profession and our medical educational system.

Further, the data from the AAMC provide additional damning information regarding the perpetuation of bad behaviors within the training system . . . that is, that *residents likely learn behavior from attending staff and perpetuate it to the students.* The 2008 graduating medical school students were asked to identify the source of any mistreatment they experienced during medical school.* In 2008, 66.3% of the source of mistreatment was clinical faculty in the hospital. Somewhat shockingly, residents/interns accounted for 67% of mistreatment, as assessed by the students! And again, no progress is being made here, as 2004 gave us 66.5% of

---

* Multiple responses were allowed, so the numbers provided add up to greater than 100%.

clinical faculty and 67.5% residents/interns as the perpetrators. While I could be wrong, one possible—and logical—conclusion of these data is that where residents and interns see behavior that is uncorrected, they emulate such behavior. In other words, as I have stated many times, such behavior is *learned.*

While we have data on medical students, we don't have data about what the office staff are asked or expected to do. I do have some stories, however, that highlight abuse of office staff. A close family friend used to be the office manager for a very large, successful physician group in a major city. The wife of one of the physicians had gone on a shopping spree the day before and had decided it would be a good idea to purchase 50 pairs (yes, fifty) of shoes. The next day this woman decided she "didn't like some of them," and she decided to return all 50 pairs. Only she didn't want have to return them personally, so she asked her husband if my friend, the office manager, could return the shoes. He obliged his wife and asked my friend if she "would mind returning the shoes." The only comforting thing about this story is the fact that, apparently, the husband and wife must have gotten along well, having the same degree of impairment in judgment and what constitutes reasonableness related to wardrobe and expectations of employees. (My friend said "No.")

In another instance, an office manager told me that a female general surgeon once became violent with her for trying to be helpful. The manager overheard a conversation the surgeon had with a patient. When the patient left, the office manager told the surgeon that there was another option for the patient, using a specific service in the hospital that the surgeon was apparently unaware of. The surgeon sat back in her chair, unhooked the beeper from her scrubs, and threw it . . . yes, hurled it . . . at the office manager and screamed "If you want to be the doctor, fine!" The beeper whizzed past the head of this individual, thankfully missing the intended target. One can rest assured that it the office manager had thrown the beeper, she would have been fired. What happened to the surgeon? Nothing.

More Physician Self-Deception. Physicians have an amazing ability to deceive themselves, utilizing a variety of techniques, and it was one of the original missteps I identified. Physician self-deception is sometimes manifested in a I-have-the-most-important-job-in-the-world attitude, reflecting an underappreciation of the fact that they are just one cog in the wheel of an interdependent, complex adaptive world.

The Arbinger Institute has published details on the phenomenon of self-deception as it relates to personal leadership.[19] To illustrate the main point, the institute uses a story about a husband and wife who have a small baby. In the story, the husband and wife are in bed sleeping when the husband hears their infant start to cry. His first thought is to get up and go take care of the baby and let his exhausted wife sleep. But then he begins to think to himself along these lines: "Hey, I work hard and bring home the bacon. And I have an early meeting tomorrow. Why can't she see that I have responsibilities and get up and take care of her kid?" In other words, he begins to *manufacture* reasons why his rest is more important than his wife's. In other words, the husband *self-betrays,* because he suppresses his initial impulse to be helpful, which he knows is the higher road.

The Arbinger authors make the point that, just before we *self-betray,* we usually have just seen something *we should do or be.* When we enter self-betrayal, we enter a box and begin to see people as objects—because it is easier to deal with *objects* than it is to deal with people who have the same desires and needs as we. Basically, it is a violation of personal integrity and respect for the individual.

Another example illustrated in the Arbinger book is the case involving waiting for an elevator that is just opening and noticing a person down the hall whom you know will need the elevator. Your initial thought is usually to hold the elevator, but, in the general hurry of the day, you simply jump on, and the doors close just before the person arrives. You have self-betrayed your original impulse to be kind and helpful.

The Arbinger book points out four key items about the self-deception or self-betrayal. When we self-deceive, we do the following[19]:
1. Inflate other's faults.
2. Inflate our own virtue.
3. Inflate the value of things that justify our self-betrayal.
4. Blame.

Some of us have developed the art of self-deception to its highest form. We are able to justify shirking all types of responsibilities, using our job as a physician as a basis for such an attitude. How many readers know someone who successfully avoided jury duty because he or she was a physician and was on call or had any other of a hundred other excuses? Of the four components of self-deception listed above, I know I have called on *inflation of my own virtue* and *inflated the value of what I do* to avoid more than one obligation, whether to society at large—for example, jury duty—or in my personal life. The attitude I copped was "I am more helpful to society by being a physician than by sitting on a jury." Even blame comes into this picture: "Well, I shouldn't have to serve on jury duty anyway—that criminal would not have committed the crime if he or she were a responsible person." In other words, I personally justify *my failure* to serve the justice system by blaming the criminal. And, of course, how much income I might lose if I sat on a jury for a week came into my thinking, too!

Over-Focus on Technical or Intellectual Ability as a Proxy for Leadership.
Cohn provides a wonderful example of misunderstanding what it takes to be a leader and confusing leadership with technical ability and knowledge: "Surgeons make excellent leaders because of the complex logistics of operations that they must organize virtually every day and the requirement for decisiveness in every operation."[20(p. S42)]

The fact that medical training is so competitive, so difficult, and so long, requiring both technical and intellectual prowess, often leads to the assumption that we are effective leaders simply because we survived and are successful in practice, because we can successfully complete an operation. Simply because you can take out someone's colon or lung cancer or diagnose their hypertension and treat it effectively does not mean you are an effective leader. Clinically competent, maybe, but not a leader.

A person's technical skill and knowledge do not make the person a leader, any more than becoming the chair of a department makes one a leader in anything other than title. Covey often describes individuals as being *trustworthy* because of *character* and *competence*. He defines *character* as exhibiting "integrity, maturity, and an Abundance Mentality."[15(p. 234)] *Competence* is defined as an individual having *knowledge and ability in a given area.* Neither alone makes an individual trustworthy. Both are required for leadership—civil leadership—because you can't be a leader unless you are trusted, and being trusted requires that you are trustworthy.[15]

Covey actually uses an example of physicians in his lectures. He asks, "Would you trust a surgeon who was competent but had no character? How would you be able to trust that you really need the operation if they don't have character? Would you trust a surgeon who had high character but was not competent?" Too often, we as physicians would retort, "I would rather sacrifice character and be competent than have all the character in the world and be incompetent." This is plain and simply a cop-out, an abdication of responsibility for oneself, an end-justifies-the-means attitude.

Failure to Appreciate the Importance of Interpersonal Relationships. The original misstep called "failure to appreciate the importance of interpersonal relationships" is absolutely critical in Misstep 3, and if 1 of the original 20 missteps had to be selected as being the most important, this would probably be it.

The ability to work within an organization is crucial in medicine. Even a solo practitioner may have to interact with hospital personnel, patients, and office staff. Interpersonal effectiveness requires personal effectiveness—that is, personal leadership and interpersonal skills. After all, we don't work with hospitals, *we work with the individuals* within hospitals.

McCall and Clair have identified 10 "deadly flaws of physician managers," but in my assessment, these apply to all physicians[21]:
1. Insensitivity and arrogance
2. Inability to choose staff
3. Overmanaging (inability to delegate)
4. Inability to adapt to a boss
5. Fighting the wrong battles
6. Being seen as untrustworthy (having questionable motives)
7. Failing to develop a strategic vision
8. Being overwhelmed by the job
9. Lacking specific skills or knowledge
10. Lacking commitment to the job

McCall and Clair also quote a senior physician executive who noted that, concerning the failure of physician executives, "It's almost always people management that does them in."[21(p. 6)] (This too, applies to all physicians, because whether we are formally managing people or not, we all must interact with our staff, our patients, and others. And earlier we learned that interpersonal skills such as those listed above are highly correlated to malpractice liability risk. At least 6 of the 10 (Numbers 1, 5, 6, 8, 9, and

10) are important components of personal leadership and can affect an individual's ability to have successful interpersonal relationships.

Our goal in medicine should be to be the quintessential example of character and competence, to personally lead ourselves the best we can—not because of what we do but because of what we are as individuals and what we are supposed to represent to the people we serve. And remember: It isn't about perfection. Rather, it is about recognition and, when necessary, correction of our behavior.

Misstep 4: Lack of Flexibility

The old guard in any society resents new methods, for old guards wear the decorations and medals won by waging battle in the accepted manner.[22(p. 27)]
—Martin Luther King Jr.

Of the original missteps, four apply here: "the physician hierarchy—the frozen bureaucracy," "quick-fix attitude," "time," and "skepticism of the softer sciences." *Flexibility* is not one of the hallmarks of a bureaucracy. The less time an individual has, the less likely he or she is to be flexible, especially when there are expectations about a certain outcome. And skepticism of new approaches and of soft data—such as when data are from a living system with complex emotions and feelings (that is, a human) that does not conform to linear Newtonian science—results in inflexibility of thinking. Always wanting to wage battle in the accepted manner, as Dr. King notes, ultimately leads to defeat. Of additional interest, of course, is the obvious fact that the antithesis of this Misstep is a Principle of Civility: flexibility!

The Physician Hierarchy—"The Frozen Bureaucracy." Hock has referred to the university system as one of the worst forms of Newtonian-age command-and-control hierarchies still in existence. He writes that universities are of a "four-hundred-year-old age . . . rattling in its deathbed and another is struggling to be born. A shifting of culture, science, society, and institutions enormously greater and swifter than the world has ever experienced."[23(pp. 13–14)] Never has there been a truer description of our medical training system.

Hierarchies are not intrinsically bad. They can provide control, stability, predictability, and efficiency when they are properly constituted and when such qualities are useful and helpful.[24] However, hierarchical systems are *always* based on historical solutions to problems previously encountered. Hierarchies fail when individuals within them fail to confront redundancy or incompetence. This results in things with which we can all identify: turf protection; departmental money battles; arguments over "autonomy" and who makes what decision; retention of incompetent, inappropriate, or stagnant personnel or physicians; and so on. The strict, inflexible maintenance of hierarchy—the kind that exists in medicine and some businesses—often leads to what Shell and Klasko refer to as a kind of "'abused/abuser' relationship between those in lower and higher positions that is self-perpetuating and mutually destructive."[5(p. 5)] The inflexibility of hierarchical systems and those within it ultimately lead to its destruction or, at the very least, to near-complete ineffectiveness in accomplishing the organization's mission. The organization self-marginalizes itself!

The shortcomings of hierarchies are something that we all have seen and are familiar with; they are transparent to most, with the possible exception of those at the top. Yet few seem bold enough to take on those at the top. How many times have you known of situations in which redundancy within the system was ignored because to eliminate it would have encroached on someone's turf or appeared to be a politically sensitive action, no matter how justified? Worse, especially in medicine, is ignoring incompetence. I'm not talking about the mistakes that we all make—the occasional lack of judgment or technical error (and I willingly admit that I've made my share of both). I'm talking about the people we have all seen who are overtly incompetent, with whom we have had enough interaction to not be comfortable with them taking care of one of our family members. The blue wall of silence that police officers are so often accused of using to protect fellow officers exists in medicine . . . because of our training and because of our unwillingness as a profession to address the incompetence and redundancy within the hierarchy. While I do believe that incompetence in medicine is not overtly common, more effective self-policing could elevate the standing of physicians in the eyes of the public substantially. It would also have an impact on liability by creating transparency with the public and beginning to shift the public's expectation away from perfection. The inflexibility of hierarchies can contribute to a leader's difficulties in moving forward. However, just because an organization chooses inflexibility does not mean the leader must.

The "Chairman's Syndrome." The "chairman's syndrome," or top-down mentality, also results in inflexibility. We have all witnessed the occasional practice of an attending physician simply stifling conversations or discussions with residents or med students by using the comment "that is the way I learned it, and that's the way we are going to do it," or the similar comment "that's the way I've always done it." These comments clearly demonstrate inflexibility. I've been out of training for nearly a decade and can still remember specific instances of such "conversations" in residency. Recall the earlier discussion concerning complexity of systems and the game of chess? There is no one right answer.

Kouzes and Posner found that managers (or, in this case, physicians) with the highest control scores—again, a manifestation of inflexibility—have the lowest scores in personal credibility.[25] One can hear the responses of some physicians now: "It isn't a popularity contest." No, it isn't a popularity contest, but all things being equal, people work harder for people they like. This isn't rocket science. Being a leader is more than a title. Paul Hawken states, "We lead by being human. We do not lead by being corporate, by being professional, or by being institutional."[26] This should be expanded by saying we do not lead because we are a physician or a chair or an attending. In medicine, perhaps more than in any other profession, we should lead by being human, flattening our organizational hierarchies, opening the gate to team-based collaborative care, and developing more flexible thinking.

The "Quick-Fix Attitude"—The Acute Care Paradigm. The quick-fix attitude, which is prevalent in medicine, results in inflexibility in problem solving and in inflexibility in the consideration of new or unique solutions. Physicians are trained in acute intervention to correct acute problems. From this they often receive the immediate gratification of seeing tangible results. While acute intervention may work in the medical arena, it often does not translate to other aspects of one's life. There are no quick fixes for bad relationships with our spouses, our parents, or our children.

There are also no quick fixes of our current leadership practice or incivility in health care. It's not like diagnosing and treating strep throat—where a quick course of penicillin will cure the problem. Sure, there are techniques that might allow one to temporarily improve some outwardly visible leadership qualities—but like giving antibiotics to someone with appendicitis, it helps for only a while. In the long term, a more permanent solution must be applied if one is to get better, and one must be flexible enough to understand the need and make a long-term commitment when that is required, with support not just from the majority of the medical staff but also from the C-suite down.

An inflexible mind-set is completely unrealistic outside the acute care medical arena, yet it is the *dominant paradigm* of medical training and medical practice today. We have all seen what such expectations translate into in some cases. I have seen physicians who were upset by not having *immediate* service at a restaurant (of which I too have been guilty). Patience truly is a virtue—one that physicians are enviably lacking in many cases. Reducing service personnel to tears is not something that one with high personal integrity does—in medicine or elsewhere in life.

The "Quick-Fix Attitude"—Time. The statement "I don't have the time" is often heard. This attitude is illustrated perfectly by conversations I had with physicians who participated in the development of a 360-degree feedback program I developed. Far and away the most common concern was "this seems awfully long for physicians to take the time to complete." It was a mere 90-minute commitment! This amount of time seems quite reasonable as the first step on a journey of potentially lifelong self-learning and improvement. One cannot expect to be able to memorize a few concepts of civility at a continuing medical education (CME) conference and have a sustained life-changing experience. This is a classic quick-fix comment, illustrating perfectly not seeing the value of the long-term investment because of inflexibility in thinking: "I know this is important, but I don't have the time."

The quick-fix mentality can make it difficult for physicians to commit to things requiring a long-term investment of time. With such intense focus on acute intervention and rapid correction of patient problems, it can cause difficulty in seeing the benefits of interventions requiring an investment of time. Enhancing personal leadership skills can't be done in one week, and it requires commitment. Reading a book or attending a weekend seminar can't teach, nor will it result in, sustainable personal leadership and interpersonal skills. There are no crash courses. It's a *life course.* It is a process that requires months to show changes, especially if the changes are to be sustained. *Flexibility allows us to control our schedules and commit to things that are important to us.*

Skepticism of the "Softer Sciences." Another contributor to physician inflexibility is a pervasive negative attitude about the softer sciences upon which much of the best leadership principles are based: sociology, social science, social psychology, management science, organizational behavior, and so on. Scientifically trained physicians are skeptical of such soft approaches to defining the world.

Einstein put it this way: "Sometimes what counts can't be counted, and what can be counted doesn't count."[27(p. 31)] Gill points out, "Understanding the applied scientific underpinnings of individual, group, organizational, and system behavior and of change management provides an excellent foundation for physician managers to develop their leadership skills."[28(p. 91)] When Gill speaks of *scientific*, she is speaking of the softer sciences, such as sociology and psychology of individuals and organizations (groups), not the hard sciences, like physics, chemistry, and anatomy. Her statement applies to all physicians, not just those in management roles.

In medicine, measurement (data) is the altar at which we worship and the trough at which we feed. But measurement can, in some cases, be merely idolatry, and it can leave our plate, if not our souls, bare. In medicine, we have the tendency to want to boil everything down to its most elemental parts; in the process, we forget about the *person*.

The medical profession *must* become more aware of the personal aspects of human relationships and be sensitive to our position and how we affect those around us. These things are not contrary to knowing and applying the science of medicine whatsoever; to the contrary, such skills are tantamount to truly respecting and treating all individuals in a manner becoming of the profession.

If we cannot grasp such soft concepts as a profession, how do we ever know a patient actually improves, in the absence of a lab test, an x-ray, or other hard data *proving that the patient is better?* If a patient says his or her pain is better, do we believe the person? What evidence do we have that the individual is better? It has gotten to the point that there are physicians who have difficulty believing that patients are improved without some objective measure.

Consider an experience I had at a large surgical meeting. I was presenting some data at a large national medical meeting—on the topic of constipation, of all things. Part of my presentation concentrated on a patient-based measure "satisfaction with treatment." I showed how strongly correlated a single question was to predicting a patient's personal satisfaction from data in more than 5,000 patients from randomized, double-blind clinical trials. One of the panel members asked, "But do you have data to actually demonstrate they were improved?" In this example, he wanted to see an x-ray test proving that their constipation was better; a patient responding affirmatively to a simple question, saying he or she felt better, was not good enough. This panel member all but ignored the fact that *these patients said they were improved.* A leader needs to understand that one is *efficient* with things but *effective* with people and that interpersonal relationships cannot be dealt with in terms of hard science and measurements but require open-mindedness and flexibility.

Misstep 5: Inability to Be a Team Player

> *I think we as doctors have to recognize that we are not omnipotent. We have to be part of a health care team, particularly when it comes to more complicated types of care. There are many other ancillary health professionals—nurses, occupational therapists, physical therapists—that are truly critical parts of the team in terms of delivery of care to the American people.*[29(np)]
> —*Gary Krieger, M.D.*

This Misstep can be the downfall of any individual hoping to be successful in any business that deals with people, including colleagues or subordinates. Of the original 20 missteps, 4 are relevant to the concept of being a team player: "win–lose education" (see Misstep 1), "physicians are autonomous," "reluctance to trust," and "challenge syndrome." In some respects, the "captive audience phenomenon" contributes to this Misstep too, although a bit indirectly.

There are increasing cries for having more physicians attend additional training to obtain M.B.A.s and gain other business experience in order to enhance leadership in medicine. Waldhausen proclaims:

> *It is my firm belief that this sort of program [additional business and management training for select physicians] will become even more essential in medicine as the transformation to the corporate model becomes ever more prevalent. . . . It is not our moral superiority but our commitment to the core missions of our profession, based on the priority of patient care, that make [physicians] more suited for leadership in medicine.*[30(p. 18–19)]

A *core problem* related to leadership in medicine is *not* that there are not good leaders at the top, although one can always be a more effective physician leader. Rather, a core problem is that physicians, on the whole, are poor team players, resulting in *their leaders have no willing physician followers* except in the most dire of circumstances. As we will see later, physicians often have difficulty selecting leaders because they, in the final analysis, are usually *unwilling followers*. Practicing providers must develop an appreciation for the power of trusting their leaders and good *followership*. Good followership, after all, is what high-functioning teams are all about. Paradoxically, perhaps, for a physician to become a good leader and to be truly effective, he or she must understand how to be an effective and willing follower.

"Physicians Are Autonomous"—A Persistent Fallacy. If physicians were to practice the science of medicine as a professional team, society might give them the autonomy they need to practice the art of medicine as individuals.[31]

Competition almost *never* results in synergy or the best performance, as suggested in the preceding section. Pursuing excellence is a collaborator's game. Competition is about making someone else inferior; collaboration is about accomplishing something superior.[25] Likewise, individual autonomy is conceptually counter to synergy and collaboration, both implying the willing participation of more than one party. Autonomy assumes that in every case the individual knows the right answers or, at the very least, can act without any controls. Knowing all the right answers or attempting to maintain an environment where we are in complete control—or even thinking we do and are—can lead one to challenge everything. Earlier I pointed out the futility of trying to know all of the answers, as illustrated using the game of chess. Challenging everything communicates that we mistrust others involved in the discussion (whether this is true or not), especially when they are subject to a constant barrage of challenge. Collaboration requires trust, and teams must collaborate to be effective.

Even our customers, our patients, understand the need for and want teamwork from their health care providers. Picker Institute research found that "Patients strongly desire a system in which healthcare professionals work together effectively, follow a coherent plan of care, and demonstrate familiarity with their unique needs and circumstances."[32(p. 1)]

Research supports the idea that lack of coordination of patient care impacts patient outcomes and increases the likelihood of complications.[33] Coordination of patient care when multiple physicians are involved provides a wonderful opportunity for a unified team approach, yet, as noted, physicians wanting to keep control of their schedules actually becomes an obstacle to such possibilities. The model of the physician as the sole provider and unilateral decision maker is broken and was never the right model in the first place. It needs to be shelved in the archives of medicine.

The concept of physician autonomy in the era of evidence-based medicine is anathema. Physicians acting autonomously results in huge variations of practice and, hence, outcome. Even physicians who practice in groups custom craft their treatment plans. In fact, only 55% of the time is evidence-based medicine used in preventive and chronic disease treatment.[34] This is illustrated by a retrospective chart review study I once participated in. The group I was with was charged with reviewing the charts of patients who had undergone colectomy (removing part of the colon via surgery) by surgeons in a major teaching facility. The goal was to define "standard methodology by which a colectomy was performed and managed postoperatively." What our research team found was shocking. We had expected variation between surgeons. What we didn't expect was that all of the surgeons varied their own practice within their practice! In other words, no individual surgeon did the surgery the same way every time, nor was the postop management the same from patient to patient!

If health care leaders allow variation to flourish in the pursuit of autonomy, with very broad evidence-based goalposts, we will be responsible for ongoing mistakes, patient safety gaffes, wasted resources, and never-ending complexity.

The provider's tendency to fall back on autonomy, especially when confronted with external change or pressure, can be used as a cloak, a self-protective form of self-deception, making it appear that physicians are focusing solely on "what's in it for me?" The quest to maintain this sort of autonomy can lead to failure to appreciate the interdependence of oneself with other components of the health care system and society at large, both being complex adaptive systems. A more fruitful approach, not only in the increasingly bottom-line-focused health care environment but also for our patients, would be for physicians to see themselves as partners with all parties involved in patient care or their business and seek win–win solutions framed by the attitude of "what's in it for all of us?"

As Shell and Klasko point out, "Autonomy is a poor fit for complex business environments, such as health care today."[5(p. 5)] Physicians can keep insisting on remaining autonomous, but only at ever-increasing costs—emotionally and financially—to themselves.

I recall an episode in my early surgical career when I clung to autonomy. I enjoyed doing critical care while I was in training and in practice, and I tended to have many patients on respirators. Early in my career, I used to become offended and incredibly defensive when the respiratory therapist would make suggestions or inquire about my orders for the ventilator settings. How ridiculous was it for me, who, from a physician's standpoint, did have significant experience with ventilators, to miss the fact that I still only had a modicum of experience compared to the respiratory therapist, who spent every hour of every day working with ventilators and difficult-to-manage patients? Very ridiculous, indeed. I soon learned several important lessons from such experiences: First, I learned how much more these fellow team members actually knew compared to me. I also learned how much more motivated they were when I began to treat them with the respect they deserved as people, let alone as the professionals they were. Finally, I learned how trusting them to do their job, empowering their expertise and motivation, substantially freed me from doing things I didn't need to be doing. Simply by giving up my false sense of autonomy and realizing that these individuals were valuable team members made all the difference in the world.

I see this same behavior played out again and again in organizations all over the country. Some orthopedic surgeons don't believe that giving medicine to prevent a blood clot from occurring in a patient's leg (deep venous thrombosis [DVT]) is necessary, so they don't order the medicine, despite the evidence that it is critically important. And cardiologists sometimes don't follow guidelines for failing hearts because in "their experience," all those bad things the papers talk about haven't happened to their patients. Critical care doctors may "overlook" the intensive care unit (ICU) staff's reluctance to provide routine mouth care to patients on breathing machines (ventilators). Each of these is an example of physicians making decisions contrary to evidence-based practices where clear data show benefit. The motivator must partly be an ill-guided desire to remain autonomous. Unfortunately, it is the patient who might pay . . . in complications or poorer-quality outcome. This type of attitude is, in essence, saying that the physician values his or her "own autonomy more highly than the patient's outcome."[35] As noted in the introduction to this section, physicians must practice science as a team in order to be granted the privilege of practicing the art of medicine.

What multidisciplinary teams can accomplish is remarkable. In one hospital, I set up a multidisciplinary rounds team for ICU trauma surgery patients. Team members included nurses, respiratory therapy staff, physical therapy staff, social services staff, discharge planning staff, dietitians, a pharmacist, and a physician, when available. A physician's assistant coordinated the group and directed the rounds on Monday, Wednesday, and Friday. The team was empowered to round on each trauma ICU patient and make and implement recommendations, whether the attending surgeon was present or not. Agreement with the model was obtained with all trauma surgery surgeons prior to implementation. Data were collected for six months, and patients were matched (case-mix index matching) to a similar group of patients from the six months prior to implementing the team. The multidisciplinary team reduced total ventilator days in ICU trauma patients by 1.4 days (7.2 pre versus 5.8 post) and total trauma patient length of stay from 22.8 to 16.7 days. This resulted in savings of more than $9,000 per trauma patient admitted to the ICU.[36] These results were obtained by dedicated team members who acted in unison and often without the direct participation of a physician. This is truly an example of what collaborative leadership and empowerment of team members can do.

Team-based health care demands respectful interaction between all team members, regardless of role. This includes committing to civility-driven, relationship-based care and an expectation of members living within the bounds of the Principles of Civility. This isn't just a bunch of nice words. There is actual quantitative evidence supporting the idea that behaviors that shut down information sharing and openness—things like intimidation, anger, belittlement, and feeling rushed— jeopardize patient safety and outcomes. Karen Mazzocco and colleagues found that "patients whose surgical teams exhibited less teamwork behaviors were at a higher risk for death or complications, even after adjusting for ASA risk category."[37(p. 682)] For more on team-based health care, *see* Sidebar 6-1, pages 96–97.

Reluctance to Trust (Nonphysician Experts). Despite wanting to function autonomously as individual practitioners, physicians share an almost supernatural degree of trust in the opinions of a medical colleague when it comes to the care of a single patient and other clinical matters. And the level of trust seems to be relevant to the institution granting a physician's degrees. This seems almost laughable to me, when, as providers, we don't generally even pause and think about the trust patients put in us. Consider this perspective that I often use in my live presentations:

Sidebar 6-1. Team-Based Health Care—Practice Time?

Grumbach and Bodenheimer note there are two key questions for teams[38]:
1. Who is on the team?
2. How do team members work together?

Simply because people work in the same office or on the same hospital unit doesn't mean they function as a team. A football team composed of the right number and type of players will have little success if it doesn't have a playbook, doesn't practice, and doesn't develop a game plan. Likewise, a group of health care providers thrown together into a clinic or a care unit can be called a team but may not demonstrate teamwork.

A team "is a group with a specific task or tasks, the accomplishment of which requires the inter-dependent and collaborative efforts of its members."[39(p. 73)] The authors who constructed this definition use an illustration of the difference between a mere grouping of people and a team:

> It is naive to bring together a highly diverse group of people and expect that, by calling them a team, they will in fact behave as a team. It is ironic indeed to realize that a football team spends 40 hours a week practicing teamwork for the two hours on Sunday afternoon when their teamwork really counts. Teams in organizations seldom spend two hours per year practicing when their ability to function as a team counts 40 hours per week.[39]

Add to these observations the obstacles of interdisciplinary territoriality in health care and the inevitable inertia of large organizations, and it is a wonder there is ever a coordinated effort!

The fact that health care rarely, if ever, practices teamwork in the same manner as a football or baseball team makes an emphasis on clear, effective communication even more important—in fact, critical.

Wise et al. have suggested that there are five elements to building a team.[39] Table 1, page 97, provides a summary of their findings in terms of key elements and illustrations. *(continued)*

Sidebar 6-1. Team-Based Health Care—Practice Time?

continued

Table 1-1. Team Building in Health Care

Key Element	Illustrations

1. Defined goals	**Based on organization mission statement (examples):**
	• Employee and physician satisfaction
	   – Improved financial performance
	   – Reduced access to care
	Measurable objectives (examples):
	• 100% retention
	• Expenses covered with profit
	• 90% of patients calling will be seen within 48 hours

2. Systems	**Clinical system support:** • Integration of the electronic medical record • Timely scheduling of procedures **Administration support:** • Procedures for checking patients into clinic
3. Division of labor	**Definition of tasks** **Assignment of roles**
4. Training	**Training each team member in the routine tasks for each defined role** **Cross-training for acute needs**
5. Communication	**Communication structure:** • Routine, via paper, online • Collaborative rounding at a predefined time • Team meetings **Communication processes:** • Open, honest, and respectful feedback • Conflict resolution

Source: Adapted from Wise H., et al.: *Making Health Teams Work.* Cambridge, MA: Ballinger, 1974.

It is not necessary for a leader to know how to do everything. It is necessary for that individual to know which team member is best suited for the job and how to empower that team member to do it without jealousy or micromanaging. Giving up the idea of autonomy is important for a civil leader . . . and for effective followership.

A patient can walk into my office and look at my diplomas, see that I am a board-certified general surgeon, and a Fellow of the American College of Surgeons. They can see I have a degree in surgery and master of medical management degree. But in reality, they have no clue whether I am truly competent! They don't know if I can really even fix the medical issue they are coming to talk to me about. What they do know, and know very quickly . . . within two minutes of my entering the exam room . . . is if they like me as a person. They develop a sense that they can trust me.

This reminds me of a conversation I had with a physician executive of one of the largest HMO health plans in the country. I asked him what he thought of leadership in medicine in general. He rattled off about five or six things without even having to pause to think about it. One of his responses was that "physicians need to learn how to choose a leader. But they can't and don't because doctors hate being part of a team and can't function within teams. I know a guy at the AMA who says that 'trying to get doctors to follow a leader is like trying to get eagles to fly in formation.'" (How does one create a team-based approach with this kind of dynamic driving behavior?) His conclusion was that physicians basically don't trust anyone other than themselves to lead them. Recalling the win–lose paradigm and the inability to negotiate, where physicians just want to make sure "no one gets more than me," reinforces this gentleman's statement. In addition, this illustrates a second problem, mentioned earlier: In addition to not selecting leaders, physicians are often unwilling to be led. In other words, the fact that physicians don't follow others is related to a lack of trust of the physicians who have actually stepped up to the plate.

Leaders not only create but also thrive in the environments of trust they must help create in their organizations. They know that without trust, not only are effective teams not possible, nothing is possible. On-the-ground providers appreciate that their most important responsibility is to others and that they are just one part of an interdependent reality.

The "Challenge" Syndrome. The "challenge" syndrome emanates from the fact, as mentioned earlier, that as providers are trained, they are taught to *challenge* everything for the good of the patient. Unfortunately, this too easily devolves into behavior that leads us to challenge everything, period. My father, also a physician, wrote me a letter shortly after I graduated from medical school, full of his considerable wisdom, warning me of this very mind-set. To paraphrase, he said "Becoming a physician will allow you to be an expert in medicine, *if* you work hard. It does not mean you are an expert in anything else."

His statement has a great deal to do with being part of a team . . . listening to and relying on others who know more than we do. If we voice opinions about things in which we are clearly not expert—and voice them with such conviction that those around us do not question—it is essentially another form of win–lose thinking. It is a reflection of a less-than-optimal ability to *listen and hear* others.

I have a friend who makes his living as a certified financial planner. He claims that his most difficult clients, beyond question, are physicians, and they are the occupation *least likely* to follow his advice. They are also the most likely to get into financial trouble from their own financial decisions. I subsequently asked my own financial planner about my friend's opinion. He heartily concurred, adding, "Physicians are notorious in the financial community for not taking advice and making very costly decisions." This is a form of arrogance, the quintessential not knowing what we don't know. Asking a question is not a bad thing; persisting to push one's point in an area where one has less experience than another is what I am talking about. It is not a good trait for a team member.

Failure to Appreciate the Importance of Interpersonal Relationships. How many physicians allow their residents or office staff to call them by their first names, as opposed to "Dr. So-and-So"? I know of very few; I encourage my office staff to call me "Mike" if they are comfortable doing so. It does wonders for interpersonal relationships in the office and helps morale immensely. I do the same on the hospital units and in the operating room. Staff feel more respected, more connected, and part of a close-knit team.

Physicians use the manner in which they are addressed and how they address others, whether consciously or unconsciously, as a mechanism to maintain authority over their world. It is an example of a difference of respect, no matter how subtle. According to Hilfiker:

> *What we call each other is symbolic. Too often the physician remains "Dr. Hilfiker" long after the nurse has become "Annette." Physicians usually perceive themselves as bosses, even though they are often not the staff's actual employer.*[8(p. 161)]

Effective individuals know they don't know it all and rely on and empower—trust—those on the team who do know the answer. They are not intimidated by what they don't know, and they welcome the knowledge and contributions of others. Leaders realize they are not experts in everything. Real leader know they don't have to be; that's why they have other team members to rely on. After all, staying firmly implanted in one's own sphere of competency is critical to patient safety and outcome.

Misstep 6: Failure to Develop Others

There may be some confusion as to why this is a misstep for physicians. After all, physicians train medical students and residents, right? Training someone in a technical skill, such as diagnosis or treatment, is not the same as helping them to *develop as a person.* Helping a person develop better personal leadership and interpersonal and communication skills requires careful observation of behaviors and routine constructive feedback. It also requires that the teacher have good—preferably excellent—interpersonal and communication skills. As we have seen from the AAMC data, in some cases, we are teaching the wrong behaviors.

The "Perfectionist" Mentality. We need to ensure that we begin to shift from training people in the mind-set of perfection to the army's mind-set of becoming the best you can be. In medicine, we need to change the way we respond to mistakes—even critical errors—to shift from blaming, belittling, and other punitive actions, to explanation, responsibility, accountability, and assurance that individuals learn how to become better and learn from errors. We need to establish *nonpunitive systems of reporting errors* and get away from the perfectionist focus.

This reminds me of two concepts that I really like and try to remember regarding mistakes. Covey has said, "Our response to any mistake affects the quality of the next moment."[15(p. 91)] How true Have you ever snapped at your office staff after *you* have made a mistake? I know I have, and the staff had no clue about what they did to cause my reaction.

Cashman states, "Failure is a subjective label we apply to unintended or unexpected experiences."[40(p. 80)] What if we began to think about at least some mistakes in medicine as performance enhancers or educational opportunities? I made some incredible mistakes in residency that I will never forget; they taught me important lessons. In one episode, I was assisting in the heart bypass operation of a man who had undergone a previous heart bypass years earlier. In the process of opening his chest to expose the heart for the operation, I felt a thin band of tissue against the backside of his breastbone. I "broke" this band with my finger, using what surgeons call "blunt dissection," a technique that can be used in a variety of situations— except cardiac surgery. My maneuver tore a small (but significant) hole in the right atrium of the patient's heart and resulted in substantial blood loss. After the situation was under control, the cardiac surgeon had a fairly frank discussion with me about technique. This particular surgeon was very good with interpersonal relationships and was entirely appropriate. I, of course, felt awful. But it never happened again, and I remember it. While this was a mistake, it was a very important and memorable educational opportunity. With his response, the surgeon used this event to help me develop as a surgeon *and* as a person. He modeled perfectly how one should respond, even in dire circumstances. He taught me that responding to errors—yours or someone else's—doesn't require yelling or belittling or berating. He taught me civility.

Helping individuals to develop, as this surgeon did for me, without using unconstructive criticism or belittlement is an art we should all seek to learn or improve. Further, such approaches don't just teach medical lessons, they also teach important interpersonal skills.

Difficulty Providing Behavioral Feedback to Other Physicians. In the nonmedical business world, giving feedback related to behavior is not considered offensive. It is, in fact, often welcome. Entire training programs in nonmedical businesses are focused on coaching for enhanced behaviors. In medicine, however, because the profession is steeped in the win–lose paradigm, virtually any criticism can be considered offensive. Much as with the "challenge" syndrome, when one's behavior is questioned, the response by physicians is often defensive in nature—or worse, the self-deceiving fallback "I was only trying to take care of my patient," a.k.a. *the end justifies the means.*

This particular Misstep, then, is really a two-way street: the likelihood of a defensive response from the provider with the behavioral challenge, and the unwillingness of the observing individual to point out the unacceptable behavior. It is collusion in inappropriate behavior without knowledge of how it really impacts both individuals and, in fact, the organization.

In this case, the responsibility lies with the individual observing the behavior. If one's internal sense of principle is in order, tactfully pointing out your observation should not be an overwhelming task. Even in the most extreme of responses, your security is based within yourself and not rocked by an insecure person lashing out.

Another reason physicians have difficulty accepting feedback in a medical environment relates to direct patient care. No physician makes a decision about a patient flippantly (at least that I know of). If any behavioral feedback given to a physician is even remotely connected to an interaction with a patient, it will likely set off a firestorm of emotion. Physicians like to think they are right—all the time—when it comes to their patients.

Marr quotes a nameless physician who says he believes physicians are suffering from the "Piñata Syndrome," which he describes as "everyone is taking a whack at me."[41(p. 20)] This is essentially a form a paranoid mistrust, which he says is manifest by the symptoms of "physician lounge grumbling and griping, sniping at medical and administrative leaders, resistance to examining best practices, and a refusal to hold colleagues responsible for their behavior."[41(p. 20)]

Hilfiker states is this way:

> *The rest of the staff will meekly submit to a lecture about an alleged mistake on their part, whereas they must find some discreet way to bring the physician's mistakes to his attention so as not to offend him. Serious mistakes on the part of the physician are not talked about except, perhaps, behind his back.*[8(p. 161)]

Finally, data support the existence of this Misstep 6, "failure to develop others." The *2000 Medical School Graduation Questionnaire, All Schools Report* from the AAMC found that 41.7% of more than 14,000 medical students either "disagreed" or "strongly disagreed" with the statement "Students were given timely feedback on performance in clerkships."[18]

Leaders understand the importance of giving honest, timely feedback in a compassionate way.

Misstep 7: Lack of Openness

The eyes are of little use if the mind be blind.
—Arab proverb

Our ability to develop and grow as a person—that is, beyond our medical interests—ideally should be viewed as the fun and exciting personal challenge it is and should be. Unfortunately for many providers, this is inhibited by a lack of openness—openness to change, openness to feedback, and openness to personal development and the time required.

This Misstep is an amalgam of "the physician hierarchy," "inability to self-assess," and "information overload." These apply here for different reasons. Hopefully the reader already appreciates that the hierarchical structures in health care are often not open or innovative, nor particularly concerned about development and growth of individuals. Lack of openness contributes to the inability of physicians to assess themselves, making developing self-growth programs somewhat difficult. Finally, information overload is relevant on two levels: First, we have limited time, and we spend much of that time wading through reams of medical literature in an effort to stay current, whatever that means. Second, perhaps we are not open to reading nonmedical material and don't develop and grow as individuals because we read *too much medicine* and not enough other stuff, like newspapers, other literature, and perhaps some self-growth or self-improvement material.

Inability to Self-Assess. *Forbes* called Marshall Goldsmith one of the top five executive coaches in the United States in 2000. He is the author of the *New York Times* best seller *What Got You Here Won't Get You There*. Goldsmith, in personal discussions with me about leadership, stated that the ability of individuals to assess themselves, and how their self-assessments align with assessments of them by peers and subordinates are of crucial importance for their understanding of areas for improvement, especially related to leadership and interpersonal skills. Goldsmith says that of all professional groups he has worked with, physicians are the group that consistently self-rates their abilities and technical and leadership skills higher than others who rate them.[42] In fact, he claims that 80% to 90% of physicians rank their skills and abilities in the top 10% of the profession. Obviously, only 10% of physicians can be in the top 10%, and 50% of every medical school class graduates in the bottom 50% of the class! Airline pilots apparently fall just below physicians, and athletic coaches just below pilots. For a real contrast, consider that only about 60% to 70% of attorneys self-assess their abilities higher than peers or subordinates rate them.

Daniel Goleman's work suggests that self-awareness is crucial to developing emotional intelligence.[43] If one is to commit to change, one must be able to see one's true strengths and developmental needs—in other words, one must be open to self-evaluation or assessment and change. Again, "We can't solve problems until we realize we have a problem of not seeing the problem."[19(p. 221)]

If individuals are not open and do not see that they have behavioral shortcomings (and we all do!), and if they don't see the pain these shortcomings cause them or others, they have no motivation to change. Even if they do receive feedback that change would help them be more effective, they are unwilling to admit they have a problem, unwilling to ask for help, or too proud to believe they can do anything wrong, there is no use even trying to give them feedback, so don't waste your time trying to change such individuals. This profile is clearly one of an individual who is not open. The very purpose of a 360-degree feedback program is to assist individuals in seeing and understanding areas for improvement and developing personal growth programs.*

While the focus here has been on physicians, it is clear that overestimation of ability is not uncommon. Kruger and Dunning state that there are three points to be made about an individual's competence in the various domains of life, in which we all operate daily[44]:

1. Success and satisfaction depend on knowledge, wisdom, or savvy in knowing which rules to follow and which strategies to pursue.
2. People differ widely in the knowledge and strategies they apply in these domains, with varying levels of success.
3. When people are incompetent in the strategies they adopt to achieve success and satisfaction, they suffer a dual burden: Not only do they reach erroneous conclusions and make unfortunate choices, their incompetence robs them of the ability to realize it.

---

* A 360-degree feedback program examines the discrepancy between the manner in which an individual self-assesses and the manner in which those around the individual perceive him or her.

Kruger and Dunning say that "the skills that engender competence in a particular domain are often the very same skills necessary to evaluate competence in that domain—one's own or anyone else's."[44(p. 1121)] Experts on this topic consider incompetent people to lack metacognition, or self-monitoring skills.

Kruger and Dunning set up a series of four studies to demonstrate their points. One of their predictions was that incompetent people, paradoxically, would be able to gain insight about their shortcomings if they became more competent through training, and thus gaining the self-monitoring skills required to be able to realize that their performance had been substandard. (I will not go into the details here, other than to state that these investigators' work is fascinating.)

The key findings of Kruger and Dunning's work suggest the following points, relevant to the topic at hand:

1. The demonstration of incompetence depends on the domain in question; in other words, one may be competent in one area and not another (for example, language skills versus social skills).
2. In order for "the incompetent to overestimate themselves," they must have some "minimal threshold of knowledge, theory, or experience that suggests to themselves that they can generate correct answers."[44(p. 1132)]
3. "[T]hose who performed particularly poorly relative to their peers were utterly unaware of this fact."[44(p. 1124)]
4. Finally, paradoxically, improving the skills of participants and thus enhancing their self-monitoring skills helped these individuals to recognize the limitations of their abilities.

Why is this research mentioned here? It is not meant to imply that physicians are incompetent, at least as related to providing patient care. However, it is entirely possible that we have difficulties recognizing our own abilities in the domains of personal leadership and interpersonal skills.

"Captive Audience Phenomenon." The captive audience effect carries over to physicians themselves and to their practices. Compared to those in other professions, physicians are risk averse related to their occupation—and not just as it relates to patient care, but also in the openness or willingness to move to other practices or other cities, to try new methods of generating business or new business models, or to quit their practice and try something else. Few would argue that compared to those in the rest of the working world, physicians have a greater likelihood of simply "parking" for their career, with perhaps one practice change along the way. While this tendency is changing—as the demographics of the provider population is changing, due to the shortage of providers, and because of intense competition, often based on paying someone top dollar, between organizations—there is still much truth to this.

Information Overload. Hock says, "We are educated beyond our ability to understand."[12] He is talking about the rate of information change in society in general. In medicine, it is even worse. Much worse. The explosion of published medical literature has virtually buried the physician who has even a modicum of interest in staying abreast of current thought in the field. It isn't like drinking from a fire hose, it is like drinking from a city's main water line.

My major interest early on was liver, pancreatic, and biliary tract surgery. I considered myself reasonably dedicated to keeping up with the current literature. Yet I found it difficult to keep up even with the three or four monthly surgical publications I received. The burden is exacerbated by having to wade through tons of nearly worthless published information, as it relates to the tangible practice of medicine for the average provider.

The emphasis on being current is important, but a legitimate question is "What must be done to actually stay current?" Realistically, there are probably only several articles published per month of true value on any one topic that might substantially influence one's current practice. Finding those articles is the difficult part. We would be better off as a profession if we targeted those few truly valuable pieces of information and then opened ourselves to reading nonmedical material, including leadership development literature found in the nonmedical business world. An individual's openness will lead to development and growth in his or her personal life—guaranteed.

We have allowed premed students to become focused on science to the exclusion of a liberal arts education. Forty percent of medical students graduating in 2000 thought humanities other than English were either only slightly important or not important at all in preparing them for medical school.[45] Implicit in the way the question was answered by students is their underlying belief that courses not explicitly preparing one for medical school are not important. Worse is the implication that medical students fail to understand how other courses (for example, ethics, sociology, theology, even accounting) might benefit their careers and broaden their thinking, especially related to the humanistic focus of medicine. Leaders understand that they need to develop all aspects of their life, balancing their work and personal life. Being a more complete individual helps us better serve our employees, patients, and family. The younger generation of providers has been demanding work–life balance. Those of us who are not so young can learn much from them.

Physicians can choose a different path—a different way to be. We can choose to be different . . . we can choose to make a concerted effort to improve ourselves. My father gave me everything I need to avoid the missteps in a letter he wrote me less than one month after I graduated from medical school. In many ways, I could have simply copied his letter and published it as a monograph instead of writing this book, for it contains just about everything a provider—or really anyone—needs to know. It is living like he suggested that became the challenge—and really all he said was to act and live with civility.

Here, for the benefit of all health care providers—physicians, nurses, therapists, pharmacists, dietitians—I have transcribed portions of my father's letter to me, dated June 7, 1987:

Dear Mike,

The main reason for writing is to put down a few thoughts which, in all the hubbub of graduation weekend, couldn't be said. I'm certain you know that we are all very proud of your accomplishments and we know you have had to work long and hard to obtain them. I fear, however, that your hard work is only now beginning. You are bound to become very, very fatigued, both physically and emotionally as your training advances. This can easily reach the point that you become cynical and incompassionate or even lead to your becoming depressed. There's no secret manner by which these can be avoided that I know, but simply being aware that they can occur gives you a leg up in handling them. Don't be too proud to seek help if these become more than moderate severity. Try and remember that physical rest is important, so "cool it" when you get a chance. Physical workouts may temporarily help the emotional stress, but not the physical exhaustion.

As you get further along, I suspect you will see people, possibly many of them, who get to feeling that they are <u>owed</u> and <u>deserve</u> a 6-figure income and unquestioned respect from every facet of society. This attitude only produces disgruntlement and I hope it doesn't befall you. I hope you are doing this because it is what you want to do and that it is a noble and honorable profession. If you do your best, you will obtain a decent and comfortable income and will earn the respect of your patients and colleagues. But these must be earned, they can't be demanded. Try and never flaunt your degree or specialty. Remember that out of your field, you have no more expertise than anyone else and having an MD doesn't make you an expert in education, foreign policy, or politics, or any field.

I wish I had some trenchant advice for you about getting along with your chief and other staff. I guess you just wing it, ask your predecessors and watch and see what works (or doesn't work). Most people always learn more with their mouth closed than with it open. I would urge you to avoid getting the reputation of being a chronic whiner, both among your peers and senior staff. There is always something to complain about and always shall be until perfection arrives. If you must complain, be certain of your ground, present it in a coherent manner, offer what you think is a good alternative and, above all, don't get mad. If you don't prevail, accept your defeat gracefully and don't hold a grudge. A good sense of humor, which you fortunately have, will be one of your greatest friends, so keep in close touch with it. . . .

Many young professionals feel that their position requires that they manifest their success with flashy cars, clothes, etc. To me, this is unseemly and makes them look ludicrous. I think understatement makes a much more favorable impression in the long run. . . .

Keep smiling.

All my love,
HJW

Chapter Summary

The Seven Common Leadership Missteps of Physicians are as follows:

1. Failure to seek win–win solutions
2. Failure to consistently demonstrate respect for individuals
3. Lack of personal leadership
4. Lack of flexibility
5. Inability to be a team player
6. Failure to develop others
7. Lack of openness

References

1. Sherman S.P.: Inside the mind of Jack Welch. *Fortune* pp. 38–42, Mar. 27, 1989.
2. Tarkan L.: Arrogant, abusive and disruptive—And a doctor. *New York Times* p. D1, Dec. 2, 2008.
3. Lesser E.: *Broken Open: How Difficult Times Can Help Us Grow.* New York: Villard Books, 2004.
4. Lynch R.P.: How to foster champions. In Somerville I., Hesselbein F., Goldsmith M. (eds.): *Leading Beyond the Walls.* San Francisco: Jossey-Bass, 1999.
5. Shell G.R., Klasko S.K.: Negotiating. Biases physicians bring to the table. *Physician Exec* 22:4–7, Dec. 1996.
6. Comover A.: America's best hospitals. *U.S. News & World Report* pp. 44–105, Jul. 23, 2001.
7. Covey, S.R.: *Principle-Centered Leadership.* New York: Free Press, 1992.
8. Hilfiker D.: *Healing the Wounds: A Physician Looks at His Work.* New York: Pantheon Books, 1985.
9. Pascale R.T., Millemann M., Gioja L.: *Surfing the Edge of Chaos: The Laws of Nature and the New Laws of Business.* New York: Crown, 2000.
10. Spohn D.: *Touchstones: A Book of Daily Meditations for Men.* Center City, MN: Hazelden, 1986.
11. Kriegel R., Brandt D.: *Sacred Cows Make the Best Burgers: Paadigm-Busting Strategies for Developing Change-Ready People and Organizations.* New York: Warner Books, 1996.
12. Hock D.: Birth of the chaordic age: New leadership concepts to manage institutional change. Presented at a leadership conference in Washington, DC, Jun.12, 2000.
13. Shannon C.E.: Programming a computer for playing chess. *Philosophical Magazine* 41:256–275, Mar. 1950.
14. Waldrop M.M.: *Complexity: The Emerging Science at the Edge of Order and Chaos.* New York: Touchstone, 1992.

15. Covey S.R.: *The 7 Habits of Highly Effective People.* New York: Simon & Schuster Inc., 2004.
16. Fritts H.W., Jr.: *On Leading a Clinical Department: A Guide for Physicians.* Baltimore: The Johns Hopkins University Press, 1997.
17. Collins, J.: And the walls came tumbling down. In Somerville I., Hesselbein F., Goldsmith M. (eds.): *Leading Beyond the Walls.* San Francisco: Jossey-Bass, 1999, pp. 19–28.
18. Association of American Medical Colleges: *2008 GQ Program Evaluation Survey, All Schools Summary Report.* http://www.aamc.org/data/gq/allschoolsreports/2008_pe.pdf (accessed Feb. 24, 2010).
19. The Arbinger Institute: *Leadership and Self-Deception: Getting Out of the Box,* 2nd ed. San Francisco: Berrett-Koehler, 2010.
20. Cohn L.H.: Becoming a surgical leader. *J Thorac Cardiovasc Surg* 119:S42–S44, Apr. 2000.
21. McCall M.W., Jr., Clair J.A.: Why physician managers fail—Part I. *Physician Exec* 16:6–10, May–Jun. 1990.
22. King M.L.: *Why We Can't Wait.* New York: Signet Classic, 2000.
23. Hock D.: *The Chaordic Organization.* San Francisco: Berrett-Koehler Communications, 1999.
24. Quinn R.E.: *Change the World: How Ordinary People Can Accomplish Extraordinary Results.* San Francisco: Jossey-Bass, 2000.
25. Kouzes J.M., Posner B.Z.: *The Leadership Challenge: How to Keep Getting Extraordinary Things Done in Organizations.* San Francisco: Jossey-Bass, 1995.
26. Hawken P.: *We Lead by Being Human. We Do Not Lead by Being Corporate, by Being Professional or by Being Institutional.* http://neweraleadership.blogspot.com/2007/06/we-lead-by-being-human-we-do-not-lead.html (accessed Jul. 9, 2009).
27. Barker R.J.: *Measure What Matters to Customers: Using Key Predictive Indicators.* New York: Wiley, 2006.
28. Gill S.L.: Managing the transition from clinician to manager and leader. In LeTourneau B., Curry W.: *In Search of Physician Leadership.* Chicago: Health Administration Press, 1998, pp. 83–98.
29. National Committee for Quality Assurance (NCQA): *1999 Annual Report: Reflections on the Past, a Vision for the Future: A Decade of Quality Work.* Washington, DC: NCQA, 1999.
30. Waldhausen J.: Leadership in medicine. *Bull Am Coll Surg* 86:13–19, Mar. 2001.
31. Reinertsen J.L.: Zen and the art of physician autonomy maintenance. *Ann Intern Med* 138:992–995, Jun. 17, 2003.
32. Picker Institute: Coordination of care: Creating a "system" that works for patients. *New Visions for Health Care* pp. 1–2, Aug. 1999.
33. Young G., et al.: Patterns of coordination and clinical outcomes: A study of surgical services. *Health Serv Res* 33:1211–1236, Dec. 1998.
34. McGlynn E.A., et al.: The quality of health care delivered to adults in the United States. *N Engl J Med* 348:2635–2645, Jun. 26, 2003.
35. Isgett D.: Presentation to the Pursuing Perfection Milestone Meeting, Hackensack, NJ, Apr. 28, 2004.

36. Woods M.S.: Unpublished data on file.
37. Mazzocco K., et al.: Surgical team behaviors and patient outcomes. *Am J Surg* 197:678–685, May 2009.
38. Grumbach K., Bodenheimer T.: Can health care teams improve primary care practice? *JAMA* 291:1246–1251, Mar. 10, 2004.
39. Wise H., et al.: *Making Health Teams Work.* Cambridge, MA. Ballinger, 1974.
40. Cashman K.: *Leadership from the Inside Out: Becoming a Leader for Life.* Provo, UT: Executive Excellence, 2000.
41. Marr T.: The Piñata syndrome. *Physician Exec* 24:20–22, Jul.–Aug.1998.
42. Personal communication between the author and Marshall Goldsmith about his book *What Got You Here Won't Get You There,* 2009.
43. Goleman D.: *Working with Emotional Intelligence.* New York: Bantam Books, 1998.
44. Kruger J., Dunning D.: Unskilled and unaware of it: How difficulties in recognizing one's own incompetence lead to inflated self-assessments. *J Pers Soc Psychol* 77:1121–1134, Dec. 1999.
45. Association of American Medical Colleges (AAMC): *Medical School Graduation Questionnaire, All Schools Report.* Washington, DC: AAMC, 2000.

Chapter Seven
Standards for Civility-Driven Behavior and Professionalism

Why should each of us be interested in enhancing our personal leadership behaviors? The main reason is to become a better person, to become a better brother or sister, mother or father. Enhancing our personal leadership behaviors will enhance our satisfaction, gratification, and fulfillment in our jobs and with our loved ones.

There are business reasons, too. In the nonmedical business world, leadership qualities and the impact that leadership has on employee morale, effectiveness, and retention are clearly apparent, yet this concept is often lost in the medical business world. As we look at results, whether good results or bad, we see a value chain connected to the four types of stakeholders in business systems. The PPO Principle states that the value chain is that the providers of health care—the "on-the-ground" leaders—determine how patients obtain results and perceive value, which predicts organizational success.[1] Maister's causal model[2] has, in essence, proven the truth of this principle.

The following value chain functions in medicine: The provider's leadership skills are translated to and throughout the employees of the organization and out through the patients seeking care within the organization. And when speaking of leadership, I mean every provider at every level throughout the organization. In fact, in the quest for positive leadership results, it is more crucial to ensure that the on-the-ground providers have the civil leadership skills (and training) than to ensure these skills in those at the top because the on-the-ground providers are the ones taking care of patients! Followership and trust of our physician administrative leaders is also crucial in these days of ever-increasing complexity. An organization's accomplishing these things will, as a beneficial side effect, result in built-in leadership succession planning and an unbroken string of effective leaders throughout the organization, as well as a civil work culture, and it will ultimately cure the dysfunctional aspects of our profession.

Other business reasons for civility-driven behavior include the quality oversight agency requirements for holding medical staff accountable for behavior. The Joint Commission clearly understands the need for eliminating dysfunctional actions. It sees clearly the safety implications of low-trust, abusive environments.

But where do we start? We start by adopting standards for medical staff professionalism and behavior, backed up by clear, concise accountability specifically detailed in medical staff bylaws. It is my belief that the standards should be a document that describes the way we want to be, whereas the bylaws should detail specific types of unacceptable behaviors and spell out unambiguous consequences. In Sidebar 7-1, pages 115–119, I have suggested standards for medical staff professionalism and behavior. Any organization may adopt these for its own use, referencing this book.

Are these rules harsh? Yes. Will they anger some people? Absolutely! Are they unclear? No! Will they help change the culture to a more civil focus? Yes. Let's be frank: Any intervention that hits the offender in the pocketbook will change his or her behavior. If it does not, then you are dealing with an individual who has a true personality disorder, and you cannot help them in the standard way.

It is time we demand civility from ourselves and hold accountable those who are not interested in being part of the new culture. The future of health care lies in a civility-driven, relationship-based environment, and we are the only ones who can demand it.

Sidebar 7-1. Standards for Medical Staff Professionalism and Behavior

Preamble

An individual's behavior reflects upon oneself and affects the individual's fellow providers and employees. Individual and collective behavior of the people within an organization set the tone of the organization, commonly referred to as the *organizational culture.* As a result, the behavior of the medical staff is the public face of [the organization's name].

A healthy organizational culture is embodied by a *civil, collaborative,* and *collegial* work environment, important in attracting and retaining providers, employees, and patients, and it is consistent with the mission of [the organization's name]. Organizational culture is crucially important in health care and has been documented to have a direct effect on *patient safety, quality outcomes,* and *satisfaction.*

In addition to the intrinsic importance of the tenets of civility and professionalism, The Joint Commission, as of January 1, 2009, incorporated new Leadership standards into its accreditation requirements. These standards require a hospital to have a code of conduct that defines acceptable as well as disruptive and inappropriate behaviors; a hospital must also create and implement a process for managing disruptive and inappropriate behaviors. The medical staff of [the organization's name] believes that emphasizing, encouraging, and reinforcing the acceptable desirable behaviors is the most effective way to eliminate disruptive and inappropriate behaviors that would need to be managed.

This document sets forth standards that are intended to further enable and maintain a healthy organizational culture at [the organization's name], driven by a medical staff committed to **professionalism** and **civil behavior** embodied by the **Four Pillars of Professionalism** and the **Six Principles of Civility.**

(continued)

Sidebar 7-1. Standards for Medical Staff Professionalism and Behavior, *continued*

Standards for Professionalism

Medical staff members shall adhere to the *Four Pillars of Professionalism,* defined as follows[3]:

1. **A dynamic body of knowledge:** There is a constantly evolving body of knowledge in clinical medicine. Our profession prides itself on remaining abreast of evidence-based practices, and we are individually and collectively responsible for maintaining our knowledge base. Medical staff members understand that the body of knowledge includes not only evolving standards in clinical medicine but also interpersonal and communication skills.

2. **A singular focus on the patient, client, or customer:** The medical staff's singular focus is patients, who are the customers. Health care is a service industry, and having a customer focus will ensure ongoing and future success at [the organization's name]. The medical staff will ensure that discussions at every level of the organization—from the patient care unit to the boardroom—are focused on patients.

3. **Self-regulation:** Professions self-regulate around formal standards. Medical staff members should be involved in every step of the regulatory ladder at [the organization's name]. Everything from licensing to credentialing to peer review and practice standards deserves the careful attention of an individual trained to review and regulate the professionals within the discipline. All medical staff members shall support and adhere to ethical and code-of-conduct parameters, both written and understood as being common civil courtesy and standards for behavior. Increasingly, health care professionals are being held to quality measures regarding outcomes and patient safety, paradoxically in part due to the profession's failure in self-regulation. Every medical staff member is integrally involved and, in fact, responsible for ensuring that colleagues are held *accountable* for their clinical outcomes and their behavior, recognizing that they are linked.

(continued)

Sidebar 7-1. Standards for Medical Staff
Professionalism and Behavior, *continued*

4. **A core purpose that involves making society better:** Professionals have a publicly stated purpose to improve society. Each medical staff member and his or her practicing clinical colleagues are bound together by the singular goal of reducing the suffering associated with illness and improving wellness. Inextricably linked to this core professionalism requirement is availability and reasonable access of customers to medical care delivered by medical staff members at [the organization's name]. Medical staff members understand that there is a moral, personal, and societal responsibility for a reasonable on-call schedule, as determined by [the organization's name] leadership in conjunction with the medical staff.*

Standards for Behavior

Acting with common courtesy and civility in social settings is an expectation of individuals in virtually all situations within every society. Such expectations should also naturally exist and be expected within health care organizations. Medical staff members at [the organization's name] shall conduct their day-to-day activities with the expectation of both acting and being treated with civility, based on the six Principles of Civility (respect, empathy, flexibility, interest in other cultures, tolerance, and technical skills).

Concepts for Accountability for Breaches of Medical Staff Bylaw Policy or Requirements for Professionalism and Behavior: The Administrative Time-Out

Reasonable attempts should be made to use collegial intervention, or the "cup of coffee" approach, to initial complaints or violations that are considered serious and/or breaches defined by policy or medical staff bylaws. Simply put, a straightforward, honest, and empathetic conversation

(continued)

---

* A *reasonable* call schedule should not, to the extent possible, materially affect the individual's ability to run his or her practice and should enable the individual to have a reasonable work–life balance.

Sidebar 7-1. Standards for Medical Staff Professionalism and Behavior, *continued*

should first be attempted. Results of the conversation should be documented, and the offender should be aware of such. Subsequent violations will be subject to administrative time-outs.

The length of administrative time-outs shall be based on the number of documented episodes occurring during a rolling 24-month period, during which time 0 is set at the time of the most recent documented violation.

First Violation
When a practitioner receives his or her first written warning regarding a conduct in question, a 14-day administrative time-out shall be instituted. Such warnings must state the conduct or behavior that is questioned and specify or refer to the applicable policy and state the consequence of repeat violation of the policy. If the provider in question is an employed physician, the time-out shall be without compensation.

Second Violation
When a practitioner receives a second written warning regarding a conduct in question within a 24-month period* from the time of the first documented violation, a 30-day administrative time-out shall be instituted. Such warnings must state the conduct or behavior that is questioned and specify or refer to the applicable policy and state the consequence of repeat violation of the policy. If the provider in question is an employed physician, the time-out shall be without compensation.

Third Violation
When a practitioner receives a third written warning regarding a conduct in question within a 24-month period from the time of the second documented

(continued)

---

* Note that the "clock" starts from the date on which the letter is signed and resets for each event. For example, a second event that occurred 4 months after the first event would reset the clock to the last day of the 14-day time-out.

Sidebar 7-1. Standards for Medical Staff
Professionalism and Behavior, continued

violation, a 180-day administrative time-out shall be instituted. Such warnings must state the conduct or behavior that is questioned and specify or refer to the applicable policy and state the consequence of repeat violation of the policy. If the provider in question is an employed physician, the time-out shall be without compensation.

Chapter Summary

- In the quest for positive leadership results, it is more crucial to ensure that the on-the-ground providers have the civil leadership skills (and training) than to ensure these skills in those at the top because the on-the-ground providers are the ones taking care of patients.
- The Four Pillars of Professionalism are as follows:
  1. A dynamic body of knowledge
  2. A singular focus on the patient, client, or customer
  3. Self-regulation
  4. A core purpose that involves making society better
- Administrative time-outs, based on the number and severity of violations, can be employed after less formal means of correcting unacceptable behavior are tried.

References

1. Personal communication between the author and David Ulrich, Jack Zenger, and Norm Smallwood, on their book *Results-Based Leadership*.
2. Maister D.H.: *Practice What You Preach: What Managers Must Do to Create a High Achievement Culture.* New York: Free Press, 2001.
3. Logan D., Fischer-Wright H.: Innovation in medical leadership. Lecture at University of Southern California, Marshall School of Business, Mar. 15, 2008.

Chapter Eight
One Foot Out of the Box and Into the Future

It is also possible that the very identity and vision of a company must be dramatically shifted, forcing leaders to change direction in ways that were never predicted.[1(p. 2)]
—Larry Levin, Ph.D.

Relationship-based civil leadership is important on both individual and organizational levels. It is a crucial component if we are to achieve the greatest degree of collegiality, quality, safety, risk management, and financial success possible in today's health care environment. It alone, however, is insufficient for saving the U.S. health care system. That will require good-old-fashioned, roll-up-your-sleeves, a little in-your-face, rock-the-boat-type leadership, couched in civility.

I heard Ann Richards, a past governor of Texas, once say, "If ya always do what ya always done, ya always get what ya always got." No other industry is more prone to continuing to do what doesn't work than health care. When we do try something different, it is usually an incremental tweak and not a potentially transformative solution. Working harder within failing paradigms just accelerates the pace of our failure. As a friend of mine, Paul Summerside, M.D., M.M.M., of the Aurora Baycare Clinic in Green Bay, Wisconsin, likes to point out, "If you are losing money on every patient, you can't make it up in volume."

Our industry is the master of ignoring the successes of other industries and resisting the adoption of solutions created for similar challenges. We repeatedly try to re-create the wheel instead of going down to Big "O" Tires and just buying what is already there, waiting to be put on the car. Solutions to health care's woes do not reside in the same ways of thinking we've used for the past 30 years. It's time to try a few new things driven by bold, Eisenhower-like leaders who can operate in complex environments, push the right buttons, and do it all within the paradigm of relationship-based civil leadership. Civil behavior is the driver of leaders at this level, too.

In this chapter, I highlight a few of the challenges our industry faces and suggest a few things that might trigger some reader out there to create solutions to some of our perennial issues. Pay particular attention to Jennifer James's work, discussed later in this chapter,[2] and how to create a road map to examine opportunities. Space is provided for you to write in some ideas for solutions of your own. Who knows? Maybe even some of our political leadership will adopt some of these commonsense suggestions and make the practice of medicine both easier and more enjoyable. Hey . . . one can always hope!

Innovation and Novel Solutions in Health Care

If you don't think *radical innovation*—really, truly out-of-the-box-thinking—is needed to solve the challenges health care faces as an industry, then, quite frankly, you are part of the challenge. To keep the industry from being crushed under the weight of rampant costs, ever-worsening access, increasing regulation, and the rigidity of "that's the way we have always done it" thinking of our academic institutions, I offer some potential considerations for the future. I suspect some readers will chuckle at these suggestions. Others will put their head down and implement them or improve on them! Whatever happens, the change will take decades and will require change at multiple levels throughout the system. We should start now.

This chapter's goal is to suggest some novel, perhaps even innovative, solutions to some of the challenges faced by the health care industry today. There is virtually no segment of the industry that wouldn't benefit from some form of meaningful change, and in some instances, tectonic shifts, in the way things work. Everything should have the target of change placed squarely on its chest, and we should fully load our quiver with arrows.

Understanding Where We Need to Go

It seems that we need to develop a road map for innovation targets. We should be looking to define the theoretical ideal whenever possible, instead of, as we so often do in health care, pasting together half-crafted partial solutions. Jennifer James is an urban anthropologist and one of my favorite authors and speakers. She has suggested that any industry seeking to understand itself can do so by evaluating its current situation.[2] Importantly, James notes that it also allows one to predict where things are going in the future. She notes that if one understands an industry in terms of four criteria—its current technology, economics, demographics, and culture—one can begin to craft a new direction for the future of the industry. Think of using those four measures as tools for drawing a road map for change by understanding the current territory.

What do things in health care look like now through James's four criteria? Revolutionary technology; intense, often-confusing economic shifts; dynamic, ever-changing demographics; and 1950s culture characterize the health care system today. Table 8-1, pages 124–129, juxtaposes the present and future of health care in terms of technology, economics, demographics, and culture.

What's This Got to Do with Civil Leadership?

The challenges, as we look at our health care road map through James's lens, seem daunting. But they are, potentially, in each case, solvable. They just aren't solvable, paraphrasing Einstein, by using the same kind of thinking used when the issues were created. They also aren't solvable in isolation of each other, without a careful eye toward avoiding unintended effects.

As individuals or organizations, whether private or governmental, begin to look for solutions to these challenges, unintended effects are a very real consideration. To the extent possible, we must avoid creating *negative unintended consequences*. This is likely not entirely possible in each situation, but in every step, questions should be asked: "What else is this change or solution going to affect? Is it a good effect, or is it a bad effect? If it is a bad effect, is the negative impact more damaging than the benefits created by the solution?"

The link to relationship-based civil leadership is actually quite simple. The amount of interindividual, interdepartmental, interorganizational, and interagency cooperation required to induce the needed change will be possible only if there is an environment of civility across the spectrum, based on relationships. In many ways, the breadth of change required and the amount of understanding and cooperation needed across a mammoth system is no less challenging than the complexities of the coordination and cooperation required during World War II: many factions, many politics, many interests, many goals, and many players. If those at the table, including (or perhaps especially) physicians, cannot act within the bounds of the Principles of Civility, it is going to be a short conversation. It is through our relationships, especially those based on trust, respect, tolerance, and the other Principles of Civility, that one becomes influential. The ability to influence people at the table is directly linked to the degree of trust placed in the individual, and we have learned in this book that the major predictor of trust is communication in the relationship.

Table 8-1. The Present and Future of Health Care

	Current Status	Future Needs	Barriers
Technology	- **Electronic health records (EHRs):** expensive; poor functionality and not user-friendly; **over-promising and under-delivering;** very difficult and extremely slow to implement; pressure for regulatory compliance with EHRs. **Return on investment (ROI) is absent** or negative, especially in physician practices. - Every organization seems to want every bit of **new technology** and the ability to provide every service.	- **Inexpensive, user-centric systems** that deliver promised benefits and can be rapidly implemented—like training someone how to use an Apple computer - **Fewer organizations specializing in higher-end services** - All organizations delivering **consistent, safe, high-quality care** based on their economic resources	- **Money/capital** to invest in anything is declining or absent; exacerbated by CMS fee reductions. EHR systems are built from the back end forward, with **little focus on the end users;** will require complete revision of system functionality. EHR expense **takes money away from more critical needs such as uninsured care;** what is the value to a technology-driven "safer system" that still can't be accessed or afforded by 50 million Americans? - **Lack of coordination and cooperation in services** driven by the irrational fear that "if we don't have the same thing as Hospital X, we will lose."
Economics	- **Largest economic segment of the economy;** poor value per dollar for the consumer - **Hugely expensive training** a disincentive for young people;	- **Achievable quality measures** across all areas, especially outpatients; health maintenance - **Dramatically reduce costs of education:** online medical	- **Lack of standardization** and coordination between groups like IHI, The Joint Commission, NIH, ACGME, ACCME, and medical boards

(continued)

Table 8-1. The Present and Future of Health Care, *continued*

	Current Status	Future Needs	Barriers
Economics, *continued*	easier for individuals of higher economic status - **Expanding number of people who cannot afford care;** access the system through emergency rooms (ERs), creating challenges in costs and patient flow/throughput - **ER call coverage; shortage of specialists** driving budgets in many organizations; physician providers in the driver's seat and able to extract concessions, even if unsustainable for the organization - **Economic disincentives for preventive health:** For example, insurers won't pay for pre-colonoscopy consults for providers to meet and evaluate the patient, which improves trust and reduces liability potential in the event of adverse outcomes. Providers are forced to choose between what is right (improving safety and lowering risk) and	schools; distributive training programs; massive expansion of student/resident positions. **Reevaluate admission criteria:** grades are poor predictors of provider quality; can the bar be lower? - **Universal health care insurance;** mobile clinics; reduce regulatory burden; **novel insurance models** such as providing low-interest loans to individuals with jobs for elective/semi-elective care. - **New on-call models;** hospitalists; surgicalists; laborists; physician "extenders" - **Alignment of the needs of payers, the risk industry, providers, and patient** - **Creation of appropriate executive pay scales and limits on bonuses** - **Require justification of reimbursement based on revenue**—assumes that	- **Quality standards are hard to define;** lack of true evidence to support/create recommendations. - Creating affordable training using online programs will be **resisted by the rank-and-file medical schools/residencies** based on questions of quality and control; loss of power, economic and academic influence; rigid belief that the best providers are the "A" students. - **For-profit insurance lobbies;** difficulty trimming back the **bloated CMS regulatory system** and creating reasonable requirements; the **public's "entitlement" mind-set** - **Resistance to paying specialists in situations that are** loss leaders, failing to understand that the programs are intended to **preserve back-end organizational revenue** - **Lack of incentive for payers; federal government's**

(continued)

Table 8-1. The Present and Future of Health Care, *continued*

	Current Status	Future Needs	Barriers
Economics, *continued*	sustaining reimbursable encounters with less safety and increased liability risk. **Huge compensation of health care executives:** The costs to the system would provide insurance coverage for millions of uninsured people annually. **For-profit insurers coupling reimbursement to Medicare** despite making huge profits and/or executive salaries and benefits in the millions. **Medical malpractice environment:** Annual premiums for a physician are in the five- to six-digit range. The next medical malpractice crisis will likely be one that literally prices physicians out of a job.	executive pay be curtailed to "reasonable." **Tort reform is a component of the solution.** The other part of the solution includes better **communication and interpersonal skills training** of physicians, known to lower liability.	**willingness to limit the "free market economy"** **Insurers' powerful lobbies will block incentives;** shareholders trump paying for actual services. **Plaintiff bar lobby will make meaningful tort reform difficult.**
Demographics	**Baby boomers/aging population**—a tsunami of individuals who are/will need care **Huge ethnic diversity;** language barriers; different concepts of	**Dramatic improvements in access to care;** must expand number of primary care providers; create a **retired physicians' medical corps** that is exempt	**The government's inability to respond quickly** and remove the government-imposed, industry-supported caps on training; **training cycle of nearly a**

(continued)

Table 8-1. The Present and Future of Health Care, *continued*

	Current Status	Future Needs	Barriers
Demographics, *continued*	"health" and "care" - **More women in health care;** workforce implications - **Critical shortages in key specialties;** government-imposed, industry-supported caps on training; inability to quickly address market needs; decade-long response time - **Unreasonable patient expectations** - **Lack of personal accountability** —the "disease-ification" of obesity - **Attitude of entitlement**—"It's my right to get whatever I want whenever I want wherever I want, and I don't want to pay for it."	from paying costs of medical malpractice insurance in return for providing indigent/free care. - As numbers of providers are expanded, **conscious inclusion of ethnic applicants** based on demographics; consider **creating schools around ethnicity** (e.g., a school geared toward Latino providers). - **Expand number of providers** being trained to offset the effect of part-time practice by working mothers; **novel job-sharing structures; online medical schools and distributive residency.** - **Rapidly remove training caps;** increase the number of six-year medical schools (where students begin right out of high school); create online training programs. - **Professional honesty and open communication about limitations of health care** - **Aggressive wellness programs**	**decade** for physician providers resulting in an inability to quickly address market needs; likely **unwillingness of organized medicine to support shorter training cycles or acquiesce or support nonphysician providers** - **Cost of creating new training models and/or ethnicity-specific schools** - **Organizational resistance to** hiring women providers who don't want full-time positions - **Combined barriers of slow governmental response and resistance of organized medicine** - **Politically charged issues,** especially around personal accountability and financial responsibility; laws such as the **Americans with Disabilities Act** hamstring aggressive approaches to, for example, individuals with obesity. We regulate tobacco to improve the population's

(continued)

Table 8-1. The Present and Future of Health Care, *continued*

	Current Status	Future Needs	Barriers
Demographics, *continued*		and limits on what can or should be provided to individuals with self-induced injury/illness - **Minimum expectation of financial accountability** for all individuals except the truly poor and unemployed	health . . . will we regulate food?
Culture	- **Lodge mentality in medicine** and training; dysfunctional hierarchy stuck in the 1950s - **Lack of visionary thinking and resistance to change** - **Legal/regulatory environment is** a disincentive to innovation, in some cases preventing it. - **Training focus almost exclusive to the scientific aspects of medicine;** little focus is on communication and interpersonal skills required to maximize patient safety and quality care - **Too much of health care "run"** by nonphysician leaders/administrators with less	- **Flatten the hierarchy; distributive training models; co-training** with multiple specialties; **standards of professionalism and behavior** with clear accountability and consequences; **multidisciplinary team-based care.** - **Providers trained in business and entrepreneurship;** more M.M.M. programs - **Revised tort law** to eliminate the universal "standard of care"; **protect and enable innovation** in medicine where reasonable assumptions and where patient consent has been clear; **massive overhaul of CMS with financial**	- **Decades of male-dominated, inflexible thinking;** "That's always worked in the past" approaches; **androgenization of women in medicine** - Current shortage of providers resulting in organizations having **no leverage for individual accountability** - Legal system and its lobbies and CMS, a behemoth political/governmental body that will likely never change - **Negative stigma associated with "physician executives"** from historically ineffective physician "leaders"

(continued)

Table 8-1. The Present and Future of Health Care, *continued*

	Current Status	Future Needs	Barriers
Culture, *continued*	complete/holistic understanding of system function/needs - **Unhealthy competition between hospitals** for "market share"	**incentive for innovation.** - **Humanistic focus with emphasis on clear, empathetic communication and interpersonal relationship skills** - **More providers with advanced business degrees**; rotations for medical students and residents with physician executive leaders—enable appreciation/respect for value of physician executive leadership. - **Creation of regional centers of excellence based on resources and demonstrated quality;** mandate by governmental regulation or through effective self-regulation	- **Communication and interpersonal skills are considered "soft" and nebulous, not "evidence based";** failure of profession to appreciate the undeniable link between these skills, trust, quality, safety, satisfaction, and litigation. - **Fierce competition for limited dollars; argument against "restricting free trade,"** even though the current system is bankrupting the system; relative overabundance of specialists.

Key: CMS = Centers for Medicare and Medicaid Services; IHI = Institute for Healthcare Improvement; NIH = National Institutes of Health; ACGME = Accreditation Council for Graduate Medical Education; ACCME = Accreditation Council for Continuing Medical Education.

Source: ©2010 Michael S. Woods, M.D., M.M.M.

Having physicians with civil leadership skills, both practitioners and skilled physician executives, at the table is going to be important. We are, after all, charged with ensuring patient safety and high-quality outcomes, and what could create more jeopardy in the system than having nonproviders "fix" the system? What's more, we, as leaders in health care, must commit to creating disruptive innovation and displace the old guard who have gotten us into this mess.

Disruptive Innovation: The New Entrant's Guide to Salvaging the System

Most innovation-intensive industries thus regularly undergo major changes, including wholesale cycling of industry leadership. But the U.S. health sector has been strikingly ossified, with the same industry leaders (academic hospitals and university medical centers) that led a generation or more ago continuing to hold leadership status today. Disruptive innovation is fueled by entrants, yet the U.S. health care market has managed to either exclude or cripple realistic challenges posed by newcomers with innovative organizational forms.[3(p. 1261)]
—Barak D. Richman, Krishna Udayakumar, Will Mitchell, and Kevin A. Schulman

In his classic business book *The Innovator's Dilemma,* Clay Christensen makes a compelling argument that real advances in industry occur as a result of new entrants into a market that can provide lower-cost technology that meets or exceeds current standards in the industry.[4] These market entrants eventually force out market incumbents and cause other players to change their game, ultimately creating market change. Few would argue that creating this kind of change in health care in the United States, getting rid of the ossified industry leaders, would dramatically benefit our system. This section provides the civility-driven, relationship-based leader with a perspective needed to enter the fray with eyes wide open and to carefully select innovative approaches with the hope of enhancing the chances for successful industry change.

The barriers to innovation in the U.S. health care systems are significant.[4,5] One of the most significant is the Medicare and insurance system, based on the diagnosis-related groups (DRG) system. Product innovators must find a way to have a new device or service paid for within the DRG system. This has the effect of limiting price competition by maintaining relatively higher reimbursement for the less efficient incumbent while minimizing the cost advantage of the innovator. Alternatively, an innovator can request its own DRG assignment, but the process takes years, discouraging new entrants and reducing, or even eliminating, the potential for reimbursement in the early years of a product. Worse, there is not even a mechanism by which new entrants can negotiate appropriate and fair reimbursement with the Centers for Medicare and Medicaid Services.

In 1989, Section 1877 of the Social Security Act, commonly known as the Stark Amendment, was passed, prohibiting physicians from referring Medicare beneficiaries for certain health services to an entity with which the physician or a member of the physician's immediate family has a financial relationship. The intent of this act was to combat physician self-referral and Medicare abuse. The amendment was expanded in 1993 and 1994, and again in 2003, each time covering a broader spectrum of health services. The Medicare Prescription Drug, Improvement, and Modernization Act of 2003 specifically applied the prohibition to physicians' ownership of and investment interests in specialty hospitals and inhibited the development of physician-owned hospitals. While these laws may have been intended to protect patients and the public interest, they have had a chilling effect on physician investment in new facilities and disheartened physicians' interest in corporate strategy, both of which were beneficial to innovation in other health systems.

The final barrier to innovation is the legal system and the effect of community standards of care. Sometimes, something that is cheaper than and maybe not quite as good as the latest and greatest is still good enough. In a health care system that is failing under the weight of its own economics, it may be time to make trade-offs.

Innovation 1: Patient-Based Accountability

Perhaps of all challenges faced in health care today, the most difficult is shifting the patient population's expectations regarding accountability, because doing so involves behavior changes and active commitment. We have created—both as a nation and as health care providers—an expectation that the highest quality of health care is a right, and everyone can have the same access to the system. There is no other industry like this. If I can't afford to eat at Spago, I go somewhere else that I can afford. I might go around back and try getting in Spago's delivery door, but I would most assuredly be discovered and promptly escorted past the garbage bins! If I don't have health insurance, I go to the back door—the emergency room—and it swings wide open; I saunter in and make myself at home until my sore throat is treated. What's more, the federal government has made sure that door swings open through passage of the Federal Emergency Medical Treatment and Active Labor Act (EMTALA), also known as the Patient Anti-Dumping Law. Every and any patient showing up at the door must be evaluated, regardless of ability to pay or how trivial the injury or illness might be. It is an example of a legislative "fix" with profound unintended consequences.

Now please don't misunderstand me to be saying that people don't deserve treatment when they're injured or ill. They do. But the system needs some accountability on the public's behalf, not just the health care system's. Further, the health care system needs to be restructured to support patient-based accountability.

For example, calling obesity a disease is a subpart of another patient-based challenge related to the desire to have every unusual feeling or errant pain, no matter how insignificant, placed into some nice, neat diagnostic category. I refer to some of these tendencies, wholeheartedly embraced by the medical profession and pharmaceutical industry, as *disease-ifying normal physiologic variations.* Should the American public be subsidizing surgery for obesity, attendant with all of the pre- and postoperative costs, care for complications, and, let's face it, the easy out? Or should money be put into structured—and mandatory—weight-loss programs that include *monitored* exercise programs and dietary counseling, with the responsibility falling squarely on the patient's shoulders? A patient would not be offered weight-reduction surgery unless he or she had demonstrated and documented diligence in the program and truly failed.

While it may seem that I am picking on the issue of obesity, the same comments could be made for heart disease, smoking and lung disease, and perhaps myriad other medical conditions that could and should be initially approached by wellness programs. Unfortunately, of all of the innovations, personal patient accountability seems least likely to be addressed.

List three improvements or modifications to this innovation that you think might improve it:

1. _____

2. _____

3. _____

Innovation 2: New Revenue Models—Novel Payment Plans for Uninsured Individuals

I believe, both because of my faith in the goodness of people and based on my personal experience, that people want to pay their debts, especially when they have been treated with respect and dignity. However, in health care, we often eliminate the low-income individual's motivation to pay by the mere action of sending them an unreasonable bill. When an individual of limited ability to pay receives a bill for a laparoscopic appendectomy and overnight stay totaling $25,000, his heart must nearly stop, precipitating yet another medical bill! If I were a manual laborer earning $30,000 a year, my motivation to pay a bill, one that nearly approximates my annual income, would simply evaporate! So what happens? The individual's family loses their house. Or they declare bankruptcy. In fact, medical bills are the leading cause of bankruptcy in the United States,[6] a fact that should make every health care provider feel nauseated and embarrassed. Dr. Quentin Young, national coordinator of Physicians for a National Health Program, stated "The paradox is that the costliest health system in the world performs so poorly. We waste one-third of every health care dollar on insurance bureaucracy and profits while two million people go bankrupt annually and we leave 45 million uninsured."[6] For the providers reading this book, try this little exercise: The next time you have a patient you want to send to a collection agency for an unpaid bill, why don't you personally pick up the phone and call that individual to let the person know you are turning her over to a collection agency? Don't want to do that? I suspect not. When the provider is placed in the position of being personally involved in the financial aspects of the patient–physician relationship, conflict avoidance kicks in, and there is significantly less motivation on the part of the provider!

So what is a potential solution for this difficult issue? First, I believe that the best solutions will come from the local community where the people who need help reside. My thought is to enlist local financial institutions—banks and credit unions—to provide *low-interest loans to uninsured patients* who have bank accounts with the organization. For example, a bank would guarantee a loan to its customer, Mr. Smith, as long as he had a checking or savings account with the bank. When Mr. Smith patient became aware of a need—say needing an elective hernia repair— he would, through the hospital's financial department, arrange for payment to the provider and organization through that low-interest loan (say 6% to 8%). Automated financial analysis (and hence inexpensive!) would be done by the health care organization to confirm the patient's income level in light of the federal poverty level, based on the patient providing a pay stub or most recent tax filing. The bank's payment would go directly to the service provider, not to the patient.

An alternative to the banking model would be a new not-for-profit entity that would, in essence, serve as a bank for the loans. Community businesses, each of which has a stake in ensuring that the community remains healthy and that the local hospital remains viable, would contribute money into the pot. Bank A would, for instance, give the fund $100,000. Perhaps a health care insurer who serves the region would provide another $100,000, and maybe the new organization would receive $100,000 from the federal or state government. From this seed money, the program would be set up. With time, hopefully including wise investment and perhaps even leveraging the money contributed to borrow even more against itself, a self-sustaining system would be created. For-profit insurers operating in the region might contribute to the effort, enabling care for the uninsured, off-loading the burden of uncompensated care by local hospitals and providers, and giving them a needed boost in public credibility. Further, it is not an unreasonable expectation that the insurer would benefit by reducing the need to, in essence, cross-subsidize care of the uninsured, and this would drive down insurance costs. The point is, there are several ways to get to the same place and provide a critically needed service while benefiting many.

There are several additional critical pieces to this model, however. One is that the health care organizations must, as noted in the previous section, *have a firm understanding of the actual costs of delivering service.* To accurately and fairly charge, a lot of fluff and guesswork cannot be in play. When this is understood, a percentage of the costs would be invoiced, based, as noted, on a graded scale pegged to the federal poverty level. The goal would be to as closely as possible actually cover the costs and, in an ideal situation, make a small profit. While this might not be possible in many cases, it should remain the goal. Simplistically, as a provider and administrator, I would rather be paid $250 on a $10,000 bill than nothing. I can still write off the other $9,750, and I am $250 closer to profitability.

The second critical piece is that *the loan repayment must be tax deductible for the patient.* Unlike the dysfunctional tax credit structure giving large employers tax breaks, this would directly benefit the patient.

The third critical piece is that the bank or credit union *loan would be guaranteed by the state* in which the patient resides, not by the hospital. (Hospitals are already getting hit hard by the costs of uncompensated care for the state's residents . . . their means of recouping costs are not as potent as the state's.) In the event that the patient defaults on the loan, and the state must pick up the tab, the state is in a position to garnish the patient's wages—again in a reasonable and fair fashion that does not inhibit the ability to maintain the household—until the original defaulted costs are recouped. The state would end up paying out fewer dollars from the indigent fund because it would be paying out only in default cases. Further, the borrower would eventually pay back the state, albeit perhaps over years. In this day of electronic funds transfer, the administrative costs of such a program could be minimized, because it could be created from the ground up, from the banking institution to the state coffers. The cost of such a program to the taxpayer (that is, state), I would proffer, would ultimately be less than the cost of signing up the patient for current state-based indigent funds, such as the local-flavor Medicaid, and, I believe, in the end would make everyone feel better and be less expensive.

Why would the state agree to such a plan? First, the default rate on loans is classically < 10%, depending on the type of loan. Corporate default rates, even in this difficult time, run less than 4%.[7] Perhaps a more reasonable comparison of personal loan default rates is student loan default rates, which are only about 5%.[8] The point is, the risk to the state government of having to pay for an individual's default in this plan is probably no greater than these historical numbers. It is as close to a zero-sum game as possible. Some of those individuals who do default will be able to pay back the state. Those who can't . . . truly can't . . . will still cost the state far less than their current Medicaid (indigent) programs.

A fourth critical piece is that the loaning organizations would agree that *the borrower would be protected from the lending institution* in the event that the borrower could not make expected payments in a timely fashion; home loan foreclosure and any implications regarding transportation, such as the repossession of cars, would be prohibited. Further, the lending institution could not require payment if the borrower's daily requirements for self and family sustenance were in jeopardy. The loaning institution, however, would automatically become the first debtor to be paid after food, home, and auto payments obligations were met.

Finally, the system could be *used for payment of procedure- or non-procedure-based care,* applying to needed medical treatments as well as the more expensive surgical-based subspecialties. A formulary would be created that would provide evidence-based treatment of medical conditions without relying on the more expensive newer treatments, where therapeutic gain is minimal and side-effects profiles less certain. This is not a lower level of care but a wiser use of resources based on longer track records of more-established therapeutic compounds (drugs).

In each potential solution, emergency medical care would be provided, and payment via the noted system would be initiated in the recovery phase, from the hospital in conjunction with the provider.

Another solution for broadening coverage might entail *bundled care packages at a fixed price.* For example, a multispecialty group might offer uninsured or underinsured individuals a package of visits, based on a clear understanding of actual costs of delivering such care, plus, perhaps, a 5% markup to allow for some organizational profit. For example, a family of four would be offered an eight-visit-per-year package (two visits per family member) for $400 per year, paid to the clinic in monthly installment payments of $33.33. While I realize that even this amount can be a burden to individuals of limited income, the benefits to them might clearly outweigh the cost. It is, in essence, a direct-to-consumer capitated care program.

The package would allow for basic laboratory work once a year, such as a blood count and electrolytes and liver and kidney function tests. Cost savings would be realized in not having to bill the participant. For the most part, it would be unlikely that all of the visits would be used by any one individual or group, which would provide additional revenue to the clinic. Individuals needing additional, more expensive care, such as surgery, could be referred to the program described above. An upshot of this kind of program would be that it provides an avenue for preventive care to be delivered on some level to the socioeconomic group most likely to avoid care for conditions that ultimately cost the health care system much more if unaddressed. What's more, it might allow some people to save money by buying only a catastrophic health plan while still obtaining annual preventive care.

List three improvements or modifications to this innovation that you think might improve it:

1. _____

2. _____

3. _____

Innovation 3: Increasing Access Inexpensively

The Retired Physicians Medical Corp

Of all the ideas presented in this chapter, this one perhaps would be the easiest to implement. Providers retire at a point in their career when they are the most knowledgeable and experienced. Many retire because they can't slow down and work fewer hours. And I emphasize *can't*. The reason they can't reduce their hours is that the cost of practice is so significant that working fewer hours is financially unsupportable. A perfect example is an OB/GYN surgeon I know who quit doing the surgery part of his practice because he wanted to reduce his hours, but the reduction in hours wouldn't allow him to cover his medical malpractice insurance.

The most illustrative example, however, comes from my father's experience. My father is an internist, and perhaps one of the best ones I've ever known. He retired from full-time practice at about age 70. In the ensuing years, he hoped to continue to do some part-time practice by donating his service to indigent clinics in the Kansas City area, both in Kansas and Missouri. He maintained his Drug Enforcement Administration license and his medical licenses and kept up his continuing medical education. But despite wanting to give away desperately needed services to people in need, he still needed to carry medical malpractice insurance. At the time, insurance in Kansas was going to cost him around $7,000 per year. Now this is a lot of money, even for a retired physician. Despite many conversations with individuals at the state level in both states, he finally gave up, as there was no mechanism for him to provide free medical care without medical malpractice insurance. How incredibly sad. Think of what the states would have saved in indigent health care costs by such a program.

The country needs to develop a system whereby retiring physicians can donate their time to care for uninsured and low-income patients without having to pay for anything except their medical license . . . a retired physicians' medical corps (RPMC).

Any licensed physician who had been in full-time practice and who has an unrestricted license would be able to give his or her time to the care of uninsured or low-income patients, without having to pay medical malpractice insurance. The most experienced physicians in the country would be providing care to those of greatest need.

Many states and cities already have some form of clinic structure provided as a public health service. These clinics could be modified to support such caregiving activities with modest investment. Agreements could be made between the state and local hospitals for surgical service coverage, whereby they provide the space and operating room personnel for surgical cases to be performed by the retired surgeons in the RPMC. The state would supply lab services, in some way, to the clinic, probably through contracts with local hospitals or, perhaps, the Veterans Affairs system in the state. The state is, in some way, already paying for such services through its Medicaid funds but would, in this example, not be paying a surgeon's fee.

The RPMC would use the low-cost (currently $4 at Wal-Mart, Target, and other pharmacies) formulary items when medications were needed. The number of compounds available are such that no patient would have to go untreated; patients just wouldn't get the "latest and greatest" drugs, which often have a minimal therapeutic gain and an incompletely understood side-effects profile.

The advantage of the RPMC is that it would improve access to medical care for uninsured and low-income patients while reducing the burden on local emergency rooms, and, in theory at least, reducing costs of indigent care programs. Improved community wellness would be realized through setting up preventive care programs, such as diabetes and nutrition clinics.

Where would the support staff come from? How about a retired nurses' medical corps? a retired dietitians' corps? It could all be built around supporting this care model and simply making it possible for people to volunteer their time. The possibilities are limitless . . . if the states reduce the burden of actually providing the services.

Home Country Medical Missions

While we are trying to improve care at home, why is it, in a country where there are nearly 50 million uninsured people and there is poor access to medical care, that so many physicians give their time to foreign medical missions? Now, let's be clear: I am not criticizing individuals who give their time to medical missions in foreign countries. What I am saying is, why don't we give our time to our own country, where medical care is also truly needed? Is a person in Peru with a serious medical problem in greater need than a person in New York?

What if the federal or state governments allowed for a physician from New Hampshire to travel to San Antonio on a two-week, all-expenses-paid "visa" to provide care in a local indigent care clinic? The government could put the physician up in a nice hotel and pay a reasonable per diem, let him or her work 8:00 to 4:30, and give them the weekend off (and no beeper!). The cost–benefit would be obvious. For roughly $3,000 to $5,000 in thumbnail estimated costs (hotel, per diem, airfare, and so forth), care could be given for 200 people over two weeks. I don't need a spreadsheet to tell me this is a win–win. Sign me up. I hear the River Walk calling me.

List three improvements or modifications to this innovation that you think might improve it:

1. _____

2. _____

3. _____

Innovation 4: The User-Friendly, Inexpensive Electronic Health Record (EHR)

The promise of EHRs being able to transform medical practice—saving lives, money, and time—has been around for some time, but the fulfillment of this promise in real-world applications has remained elusive due to many factors. Among the most frequently cited are cost of implementation, privacy and security.[9]
—User Centric, Inc.

This section is the civil leader's guide to understanding what an EHR should look like from the user's perspective, and it gives conceptual guidance as it relates to implementation. It begins with some background and finishes with an outline of something that any organization could create, at much less cost than what is currently required from commercial vendors.

Of everything in health care that costs too much money for too little value, the EHR is rapidly ascending to the top of the list. For all the crap that the pharmaceutical industry gets from the public, it has at least provided significant value and improvements in health care quality, usually documented in outcome studies of sufficient rigor. Unfortunately, despite lofty promises, the same cannot be said of EHRs and their vendors. Health care organizations are spending billions of dollars—some on their own volition, and some based on impending federal requirements—on information technology (IT) systems. The focus is to improve patient safety and quality, achieved through a variety of nearly ethereal mechanisms promised by EHRs. All of this is occurring at a time when tens of millions of Americans can't even access the health care system. The IT initiatives are intended to make the system safer, but what's best? A safer system, but only for those who can afford to access it? Or basic care for all Americans, delivered in the current system? Personally, I would vote for the latter, even though I am a believer that IT can eventually help us immensely.

What frustrates me the most about the current major EHR systems is that *user-friendliness* cannot be used in the same sentence as *EHR*. I'm not a passive observer of the EHR vendors; I have piloted many of the most best-known systems. The systems that I have reviewed are cumbersome, nonintuitive, and complex. And you can have this, too, for a mere $25 million investment and annual maintenance fees in the millions!

As with so many things, many systems were not built with the end user in mind but built by IT gurus who know how to make a system to capture and retrieve data. This is virtually the only explanation for how we got where we are today.

The federal government has conspired in the promotion of these systems to the detriment of many health care organizations, just like it has stopped the health care profession from responding to the market needs for more providers by setting caps on training. By laying down requirements, the federal government has created an urgency in which billions of dollars are being spent on IT *every year* to meet the impending standards, when no system exists that can be implemented quickly and relatively easily and that is as intuitive to use as, say, an Apple computer.

The major EHR vendors should all buy a copy of the book *Don't Make Me Think* by Steven Krug and take many of his simple tenets to heart.[10] The focus of the book is making things on the Internet easy to use, as summed up by his wife's attitude: "If something is hard to use, I just don't use it much." He boils it down to a simple question: "Does a task require me to think about or question what I am supposed to do?" Every question we have regarding the "what to do" adds to our cognitive workload. When you force a user to think about something that should, in essence, be relatively easy, you squander the user's patience and goodwill.

I would love to spend the entire chapter on Krug's key points, but there are three that especially illustrate shortcomings of the EHRs that are currently available, from a user's perspective. Krug uses the Amazon Web site (http://www.amazon.com) as an example of a superiorly designed site that creates an easy user experience. The key, in his opinion, is the way that Amazon used tabs to make navigating its site easier. He points out three important attributes:

One: The tabs are drawn correctly. The graphics create the visual effect that the active tab is in front of the other tabs. In other words, they really feel like tabs.

Two: The tabs are color coded. Amazon uses a different color for each section of the site, and the other elements on the page are the same color. In other words, if the tab is purple, other navigational elements on the page are also purple. Think of the paper medical record and the colored tabs for H&P, Lab, X-Ray, etc.

Three: There is a tab selected when you enter the Amazon site. If a tab isn't immediately available, you don't know where you are, and the tabs lose their effect in the first few crucial seconds of the user's experience.

Why we have usability challenges in EHRs when there are individuals like Krug around to help us puzzles me.

User Centric, Inc., based in Oakbrook Terrace, Illinois, published a white paper on usability in February 2009.[9] It presents data documenting that "Usability is rarely mentioned by name as a barrier to EHR adoption by respondents at these group practices; yet, two of the top five barriers to implementation are related to the usability of EHRs."[9] In brief, usability is a major factor in implementation—and failure—in EHR programs. User Centric defines *usability* as "effectiveness, efficiency, and satisfaction with which the intended users can achieve their tasks in the intended context of product use."[9] Of these three usability criteria, *effectiveness* may be the most important. In brief, effectiveness is the percentage of users who can successfully complete a task. A task is not completed successfully if errors are made, even if an error is corrected. For example, if an individual is creating a new appointment for a patient but has to revise or back up from a point in the process to correct something, it is not effective. Any of you who have been shown an EHR know that showing someone a task once is usually not enough for them to avoid errors.

What about efficiency? *Efficiency* is the amount of time required to complete a task. Ever hear an EHR user complain about getting his or her work done too fast because the system was just too good? I think not. I know a pediatrics group that implemented a commercially available EHR, and the group's productivity dropped by 50%. Eighteen months later, the productivity had still not recovered, and the group scrapped the whole thing. Can you imagine the cost to the practice?

Finally, there is satisfaction, which is, admittedly, subjective. Again, have you ever heard a EHR user gushing about how wonderful it is to work with an electronic record? Not really something I have heard uttered in places I've been or visited. Surely this tells us something.

In the best IT article I have ever encountered, David M. Upton and Bradley R. Starts describe their concept of "radically simple IT."[11] In brief, they note that instead of organizations focusing on building systems that are legacy from the day they are turned on, "we can and should develop systems that can be improved—rapidly and continuously—well after they've gone live."[11] They repudiate the common mantras of the health care EHR vendors regarding implementation. The usual scenario recommended is either the "big bang" approach to implementation, where everything in current existence is replaced once as the new system is rolled out, or the incremental implementation approach, where small pieces of the current system are replaced over time.

Upton and Start note that enterprise IT systems often fail for predictable reasons. Not surprisingly, the recent history of EHR implementation failure riddling the landscape is illustrated perfectly by Upton and Start's list:

- It is difficult and costly to map out all system requirements before a project starts because people often cannot specify everything they'll need beforehand.
- Unanticipated needs always arise once a system is in operation.
- Persuading people to use and "own" the system after it is up and running is much easier said than done.

Having been on a selection and implementation team for the EHR system of a large hospital, I can personally attest that each of these factors is not only true but plays a huge role in the dynamics of the process, from start to finish.

In their article, Upton and Start describe *path-based IT principles*. Table 8-2, pages 144–145, lists these principles and provides a brief description of each. The path-based IT approach avoids the three problems noted above, and it is faster and less expensive!

In 2004, tired of paying transcription costs in a small practice and interested in IT and the potential for greater legibility and possible data capture advantages, I designed a simple EHR based on Portable Document Format (PDF) forms. Most computer users are familiar with PDFs due to the popular free program Acrobat Reader, from Adobe Systems (http://www.adobe.com). Interestingly, in retrospect, I came close to creating a modular platform, as described by "Radically Simple IT." As I began to use the simple history and physical exam form in clinical practice, I started getting unsolicited positive feedback from my anesthesia and nursing colleagues, with comments like, "Wow! This is great. It makes so much sense, and it is so easy to read."

These encouragements led me to think more deeply about EHR. From a few simple forms, I began thinking about a larger but still simple system, based on a form-like approach. Box 8-1, page 146, lists some of the forms I have created in a modular system. I subsequently began having discussions with IT developers, describing what I envisioned as a PDF–based, modular EHR. And, for the most part, this system meets all the criteria for usability. The advantages of such a system are compelling (*see* Box 8-2, page 147).

Box 8-3, page 148, lists the high-level requirements of a PDF–based EHR system.

Table 8-2. Path-Based Information Technology Principles and Features

Principle	Features
1. Forge together (not just align!) business and IT strategies.	• IT leaders often don't understand the business, and business leaders often treat IT staff as second-class service providers. • When an organization adopts a packaged software system, it is likely to end up adapting the business to the software, including sacrificing idiosyncratic but powerfully competitive strategies. • Make sure IT understands the business before starting planning. Business managers need to understand what IT can do.

2. Employ the simplest possible technology.	• Design the system with as few standards as possible (for example, network protocols, operating systems, platforms), preferably one of each.
	• Use minimal standards. Standardization of a small set of parts is critical to a path-based approach to IT infrastructure:
	  – It reduces complexity.
	  – It deepens specialized expertise.
	  – It increase the ability to reuse elements of the system.
	
	These things accelerate development, lower maintenance costs, require less time for ensuring quality, and free up time to develop new functionality.

3. Make the system truly modular.	• Modularity means clearly specifying interfaces so development work can take place within any one module without affecting others. • True modular architecture allows designers to focus on building solutions to local problems without disturbing the global system. • Modularity allows speedier development. • Modularity lower costs and reduces the impact of a single point of failure.

(continued)

Table 8-2. Path-Based Information Technology Principles and Features, *continued*

Principle	Features
3. Make the system truly modular., *continued*	• The modular approach: – Enables easy scale-up and expansion into new activities – Makes it easier to serve the needs of the organization as it grows – Avoids overbuilding capacity before it is needed
4. Let the system sell itself to users.	• Most systems fail because the people who have to use them don't see compelling reasons to use them. • The goal is to *build a system that users willingly embrace!* – If the system is universally hated long past the "get to know you" stage, it is likely that the system needs significant improvement or should be scrapped. • Keep the old interface "look," except where "new" information is needed, forcing the user to view the new screen to enter new data, before completing the interaction on the old interface. When the system has been used a while, the user is accusstomed to seeing the new interface screen, at which point you can scrap the old interface.
5. Enable users to influence future improvements.	• Any continuous improvement effort will fail without the committed involvement of users. • Actively solicit input and make sure people feel that their input matters; otherwise, they quit giving input – When an issue has been addressed, feedback should be provided to the employee or customer who raised it.

Source: Adapted from Upton D.M., Starts B.R.: Radically simple IT. *Harv Bus Rev,* Mar. 2008. http://hbr.org/2008/03/radically-simple-it/ar/1 (accessed Feb. 6, 2010).

Note: An organization that applies these principles in developing an EHR will end up with a usable system. Unfortunately, there are few commercial systems that fulfill these principles.

Box 8-1. Simple Forms in a PDF–Based EHR System

- Intake/demographics form
- History and physician form (modular design could be based on specialty need)
- Consultation form
- Clinic notes/follow-up form
- Postop notes
- Referral form
- Discharge summary
- Prescription pad form
- Billing/invoice form
- Lab requisition form (x-ray, pathology)

Source: © 2010 Michael S. Woods, M.D., M.M.M.

Not everything about the PDF system described here would be perfect. There would be drawbacks and limitations, but the same glitches exist in all EHRs. The most obvious is that forms are invariably generic, regardless of how detailed they are. Not every patient will have medical problems that can be neatly captured by a standard form. In these situations, the provider would need to enter free text, something that individuals are loath to do. But it is inescapable in an IT world trying to adapt itself to the individuality of a patient . . . a virtually impossible feat.

I am hopeful that consumer-based approaches will end up driving significant change in the health care IT arena. Wal-Mart has begun a big push to provide its employees with an easy-to-use personal health record (PHR).[12] The system automatically pulls in information from the databases of participating pharmacies, insurers, and other parties, storing this information in a password-protected digital file that only the employee can access. The effort has been funded by Wal-Mart, Intel, and other companies. The creator of the system, Dossia (http://dossia.org), a nonprofit organization, sells its software to companies for their employees' use. Information provided from such PHRs can, in theory, provide health care providers with more accurate information on a patient than can the paper forms so often completed during the five minutes before an appointment. The patient can print out the information and give it to the physician. Not only does it save time, but this system reduces the likelihood of missing a

Box 8-2. Advantages of a PDF–Based EHR System

1. PDFs can be shared with any other end user (for example, any hospital, consultant, referring physician, patient) with a free download, Acrobat Reader from Adobe Systems. No other software is needed to view or read the document.

2. It is far more affordable than other EHR systems. Using the forms would require the user to purchase only Acrobat Standard/Professional (or equivalent) and the electronic medical record (EMR) package. Affordability is the biggest EHR hurdle for small offices, and small offices are the biggest untapped market, due to expense.

3. PDF security satisfies federal security requirements (for example, Health Insurance Portability and Accountability Act [HIPAA]).

4. PDFs are usable across operating systems. The computer system and native software already owned by a user would work without additional capital equipment costs. Purchasing a scanner may be the extent of purchasing needs.

5. Data from PDFs can be collected in back-end databases that provide search/find capabilities.

6. PDF forms are paginated. In other words, a form flows like a book. Even in this day of the Internet, we think in terms of "pages" and understand what a page is.

7. Users could purchase just the modules that they would find useful. New users would be advised to implement only the Demographics module initially, which would include information for billing, allergies, and medication reconciliation. As users became familiar with the form functionality and design, implementing additional modules would be easier because the modules are all built on the same design.

Source: © 2010 Michael S. Woods, M.D., M.M.M.

Box 8-3. Required Capabilities/Needs of a PDF–Based EHR System

1. The system must be able to allow single or multiple users to access data from a database on a local drive or server, and preferably both.
2. The system must be able to search/find by patient name and Social Security number and birthday, and it must be able to pull up the EHR and any document within the patient's file. all documents need to be linked and accessible from any page within the entire EHR.
3. The system must be able to print a record in total or by component.
4. To satisfy HIPAA requirements, the system must prompt for an electronic signature and password access upon opening the system.
5. The system must have the ability to scan and import paper files into appropriate "tabs" (for example, paper reports from the hospital, labs, etc.).
6. The system must be able to securely e-mail and/or fax files from within the EHR system (for example, prescriptions to pharmacies).
7. A dynamic form for billing should auto-populate with relevant billing codes.
8. The system must have built-in reminder and warning systems that can send reminders to the user(s) via automated e-mail or pop-up windows, based on dates or values (for example, a pop-up window that would automatically remind the user of a patient that needs follow-up in XX months or years). Allergy alerts also need to be built in.

Source: © 2010 Michael S. Woods, M.D., M.M.M.

medication or failing to remember a heart condition or surgery from the past. More accurate information promotes better treatments and, hopefully, better outcomes.

While Dossia is intended to be a PHR for patients to furnish to their provider, I can imagine a scenario in which the system could be used to import the electronic information into a physician's or an organization's own simple EHR. In an ideal world, information updated by the patient or physician would be reflected in the other system, further reducing the potential for error.

List three improvements or modifications to this innovation that you think might improve it:

1. _____

2. _____

3. _____

Innovation 5: Civil Leadership Training

An expectation for training health care providers in the Principles of Civility with the goal of creating an army of relationship-based civil leaders must, of course, accompany this book. From top to bottom, standardized training should be implemented, beginning in medical school and targeting all individuals right on through to attending physicians. And no, sorry, there is no grandfather clause.

What does the training look like? First, the content addresses the Principles of Civility and likely is online. In medical schools, ethics courses—already part of the curriculum—will reinforce the principles. Tests will be given, and the simple concept of "demonstrates (or acts with) the Principles of Civility" will become a line item to which a grade is assigned on every clinical rotation.

For practicing physicians, the online training or, alternatively, live seminar-based education will be required at initial appointment to the medical staff, and a refresher course will be offered every other or every third year. The clinical chair will assess, based upon feedback from colleagues, how each member is "demonstrating the Principles of Civility" as part of an annual assessment for clinical quality. Practicing physicians will be required to submit, as part of the requirements for recertification, their "grades" on living civilly. Anyone with marks averaging worse than a "C" (or average) on this behavioral measure would be required to participate in some remedial program prior to taking the recertification exam.

Additional assessment of provider behavior could be obtained through 360-degree feedback tools. Such tools ask a variety of questions of the participating providers, such as ranking how they view their abilities on "Seeking win–win solutions." Each provider would also be ranked on the identical items by those he or she closely works with, such as nurses, students, residents, and fellow staff providers. If a provider thinks he is "Particularly effective" at "Seeking win–win solutions," but his coworkers think he has "Average effectiveness," the provider would be manifesting overconfidence in his ability on this particular skill. This, in essence, represents a disconnect from reality and an opportunity for improvement. A 360-degree tool could be built around the Principles of Civility. A tool has been developed to assess providers on the Seven Common Leadership Missteps and is commercially available.*

List three improvements or modifications to this innovation that you think might improve it:

1. _____

2. _____

3. _____

Innovation 6: Increasing Access, Part 2—*Online Medical Schools and Distributive Training*

Let's face it. We simply can't react quickly enough to the market need to increase the number of physicians. Real innovation is needed to address the access issues the U.S. health care system confronts, and provider leadership is critical.

The University of Phoenix is the largest university system in the world. During its development, many naysayers criticized the organization, saying it would never work. Today, such statements, in retrospect, seem patently foolish. Why can't there be a University of Phoenix Medical School?

There is virtually nothing that I learned in the first two years of medical school that I couldn't learn from well-designed online curricula. Class discussions would occur via online bulletin boards and real-time chat class sessions. E-mail would be an avenue for questions to the professor. Great, you say, but what about the clinical years? No sweat. The university can identify practitioners in the community in which the student resides and arrange for clinical rotations with private practitioners or local hospitals. The curricula for the basic rotations—family medicine, internal medicine, general surgery, OB/GYN, pediatrics—would be

---

* LeadeRx is a 360-degree multirater feedback tool for providers, available from Civility Mutual Educational Services. *See* page 163 for more information.

standardized, downloadable booklets, based on evidence-based practices, where available. For specialty rotations, such as a cardiology or neurosurgery rotation, the student might have to travel to a nearby community. The clinical faculty would have to be board certified in their specialty and would be volunteers. Grading would be done online by the instructor, and standardized postrotation exams would be given online; minimum scores would be expected.

Graduates from the online medical school would participate in the residency match, just like other medical school graduates. But the number of programs would be expanded by using the same community distributive model described above. For example, community, non-university-based surgeons would agree to participate and would have a resident for a defined period of time. Residents would be required to spend a set period of time with a defined number of different surgeons to ensure broad exposure to technique, pathology, and clinical situations. Predefined subspecialty rotations would be mandatory, such as six months on cardiovascular surgery and three months on neurosurgery. All specialties would have similar structure.

The basic point is that we could respond much more quickly to market demands and the need for increased access to care by quickly expanding the number of graduates with online training. Such approaches have been shown to be successful in many other industries, and there is no reason this can't be done in health care.

There is an added attraction to this model: cost. The cost of education in medicine is getting out of hand, with students graduating with six-figure debt in an environment of ever-declining reimbursement. This model would *dramatically decrease the costs of training* by reducing the personnel required to run a program, as well as the costs of the physical assets of a physical medical school. The assets required for the clinical years already exist, resulting in essentially no added costs.

List three improvements or modifications to this innovation that you think might improve it:

1. _____

2. _____

3. _____

Innovation 7: Building Teamwork into the System

Co-Training Schools: Creating Respectful Multidisciplinary Teams Early

Physicians need to get over it: The old model of "I'm in charge, captain-of-the-ship. Damn the torpedoes!" is broken, and frankly, it was broken from the outset. We train in professional isolation, a perfect model for developing, well, people well positioned to not be team players. If we want to shift the way physicians think about their co-providers, we need to get providers-in-training into their shoes. And vice versa.

Medical and nursing students and other health care providers-in-training, such as physical therapists, pharmacists, social workers, and dietitians, need to start training together. Why not have some core classes during the training period *with* each other? Have relevant anatomy, physiology, and pathology classes taught together. Allow the students to get to know each other, outside the local watering hole. In the clinical years, pair groups of medical students with groups of nursing students and pharmacy students and therapists and dietitians to conference about patients. Have a skilled provider facilitate (regardless of title or job function) the multidisciplinary sessions so that each functional group gains an understanding of the others.

In a sense, the goal would be to create expectations of respect . . . of the individual and of the competencies of the functional area. The medical student and resident would learn to respect what the nurse, dietitian, and physical therapist can add. A team-based approach focused on collaboration, communication, and mutual respect would drive all functional groups' training. Even though we know a resident will likely practice somewhere else in a geographic sense, he or she will carry "respect by proxy." He or she will have developed a respectful appreciation for nonphysician colleagues that will, hopefully, transcend titles and turf.

List three improvements or modifications to this innovation that you think might improve it:

1. _____

2. _____

3. _____

Innovation 8: Novel Staffing/Recruiting/Retention Models

The Over-Recruit, Overpay Strategy

Declining reimbursement from all payers places extra stress on the system for both providers and health care organizations. As busyness increases and fatigue sets in— mental, emotional, and physical—providers respond by either electively limiting their clinical volume (to maintain work–life balance) or demanding increased incomes, regardless of the actual practice revenue generated. This will be increasingly true of hospital-based employed providers because health care organizations rely on them as the source of revenue generation. Organizations will have to make choices between paying providers incomes above supportable market rates or accepting the churn of constant turnover and interval productivity losses, as competing organizations raid their provider groups with even better offers. In the end, it is my belief that the health care organizations that will win in the next two decades are those that will over-recruit compared to actual demographic need while relatively overpaying the revenue-generating specialties. This strategy will be required in order to ensure that providers maintain their desired work–life balance, especially related to on-call requirements, at a high enough income to dissuade them from leaving for better financial deals at competing organizations.

Novel Call Structures

Imagine that you are a busy general surgeon, with a booming elective surgical practice. The hospital, to which you have been dedicated for the past 15 years, requires all active medical staff to participate equally in on-call coverage. You are on call once every four days. Your busy OR schedule day is today, a Wednesday, and you have six surgeries scheduled. Halfway through your first gallbladder surgery, the ER calls and needs you to see a patient with abdominal pain. You finish the surgery and run down to the ER. The patient has a perforated colon from diverticulitis, and is septic. You decide to take the patient to the OR urgently, and you delay your second case. Three hours later, you emerge from the OR, tired and upset that you still have five cases left, and it is already 11 A.M. You potentially just saved the life of the individual from the ER, but you don't have time to even pause and reflect. During your fourth case, the ER calls again, about a patient with appendicitis. You add this case on at the "end of the day," which is now looking like late evening. At 3 P.M. the staff changes to the late shift, and you keep them busy until 11 P.M., at which point the on-call crew comes in to finish your day. Another patient is in the ER with gallbladder pain and gallstones. You are so tired, you decide to admit the patient, control her pain with narcotics, and figure out when you can do her surgery sometime in the next two days. You finally get home at about 3 A.M. and collapse into bed. The alarm goes off at 6:30 A.M., and you climb out of bed, exhausted, and head to work at 7:30. After rounding, you call the office and tell them to cancel or move the last two hours of your clinic, because you are at the end of your rope.

The following week you are on call again, but it is your clinic day, and you have 35 patients scheduled. At 10 A.M., the ER calls. A critically injured patient is being brought to the ER and will be there in 10 minutes. The trauma team is being activated, and you are the surgeon. You walk to the hospital, fuming over having just canceled your clinic up until noon, and maybe all day. The patient with gallbladder disease is scheduled for surgery late the following day, so she is staying in the hospital yet another day that isn't medically needed but is necessary because of unwieldy schedules and the human limitation of exhaustion.

In each of these cases, the surgeon (and the hospital) is losing revenue and, in many cases, health quality, due to the on-call burden. He is losing money because of the dynamics of the call situation. Canceling patients in clinic is like canceling all surgery next week. And in the real world, in the vast majority of cases, there isn't a resident to pick up the slack. What is perhaps even worse in this very real scenario is that staff and patients become angry. Imagine being one of the patients of this surgeon, scheduled electively four weeks ago, having had nothing to eat or drink since midnight, and now your 10 A.M. surgery is starting at 6 P.M.

There is perhaps no issue more contentious than call. Whether for a critical access hospital or an urban trauma center, covering emergency services is a really big deal, is increasingly hard to do, and is almost always expensive. The need for ER services has burgeoned, increasing by 26% between 1993 and 2003.[13] Access to care is further exacerbated by the fact that during this same time, 425 ERs closed their doors.[14] My own specialty society, the American College of Surgeons, has published the "Statement on Emergency Surgical Care," which includes the language "the responsibility of all surgeons, regardless of their practice, to participate in their local system of emergency surgical care in order to provide for the health of the public."[15] It is so vague in its construction as to be almost pointless.

Maa and coauthors point out that much of what is being observed in the United States is a "mismatch in supply and demand."[14(p. 10)] They note that there is a shortage of "key on-call specialists willing to take emergency calls,"[14(p. 10)] including neurosurgeons, orthopedic surgeons, and general surgeons. While they list a series of solutions, specifically absent from their suggestions is actually increasing the supply of the pool of providers by expanding the number we are training. They speak of rising costs of uncompensated care, declining reimbursement, malpractice costs, and lifestyle considerations. Their article outlines their program at the University of California, San Francisco, an academic medical center. It goes without much need to say that the model is of limited value outside academia, where there is not a supporting choir of residents. It is, in fact, an illustration of a barrier to meaningful innovation, where the same ossified industry leaders of the past (academic hospitals and university medical centers) create solutions whose relevance is not transferable to the whole. It isn't that it isn't good work . . . it just doesn't work outside Mecca, where the rest of us live and work.

So what do the rest of us do? Just suck it up and take our lumps? The answer depends on many variables, and there are likely multiple solutions, and, I think I can say with confidence, there is no single best solution. What I do know is that novel solutions will need to be built around different revenue–cost models, with the goal of preserving the major revenue drivers of the institution. Usually, this means focusing on throughput in general surgery, orthopedics, and other procedure-related specialties. Further benefits may be gleaned from more efficient use of personnel, particularly OR staff, as well as reducing extra hospital days for individuals who must wait in the hospital for a procedure that can't be completed for another two days.

The most difficult challenge is not larger medical organizations in urban centers. Rather it is smaller hospitals with limited staff. A critical access hospital with one or even two general surgeons is, in many ways, a very difficult issue. Being on call every night or every other night is a substantial burden, even if there is not much going on. The mental effects of constant availability become an ever-present drag and are an important lifestyle-altering situation. Yet a surgicalist program is not a likely scenario in these hospitals. In these situations, the hospitals that will win in the long run will use the over-recruit and overpay strategy mentioned earlier in this chapter. Using this model, they could create a stable staff of, for example, general surgeons. While paying the surgeons an income that may not be justified by the total group productivity, the back-end organizational revenue would more than cover the shortfall of the actual practice. For example, a small hospital may have the demographics to support only two general surgeons. The organization, however, has had difficulty maintaining a stable surgical practice, consistently losing surgeons due to the every-other-day call schedule. This organization would hire not one but two new surgeons, for a total of three, in order to create a call schedule that allows a more reasonable work–life balance and helps maintain or even grow surgical volumes. All of these surgeons would be placed on a salary guarantee, with a minimum productivity threshold and incentives upon reaching a prespecified work-related value unit (WRVU). Stabilization of the surgical practice would occur, and the back-end revenue for the hospital would be secured.

In larger hospitals, a separate program would be devised, based on ER visits and urgent care requirements. Maybe a single surgeon could perform a surgicalist role 7:30 A.M. to 4:30 P.M., Monday through Friday, relieving busy, revenue-generating elective general surgeons to do their clinics and elective cases. At 4:30, the surgicalist would go off service, and the elective surgeons would rotate through a call schedule. They would round on all surgical inpatients and handle inpatient consults. They would coordinate multidisciplinary surgery rounds. Patients admitted by the on-call surgeon during the wee hours of the morning for things like gallbladder disease could be operated on by the surgicalist the following day if there were open OR spots, assisting in inpatient bed availability. In fact, the surgeon admitting such a patient would automatically list the patient for surgery, knowing that the surgicalist would be picking up the case in the morning. No more surgical cases would be delayed for two days because the on-call surgeon's schedule is fully committed or he or she is exhausted. Not only would this free up an inpatient bed at least a day earlier, it would prevent having to call in after-hours staff to do what is, in essence, elective surgery. The surgicalist, assuming that another surgeon had not operated on the patient, would provide postdischarge follow-up. If the surgicalist were called away from the clinic, the elective general surgeons would pick up the clinic patients. The benefits of a surgical service as described here are outlined in Box 8-4, pages 157–158. In any situation where there would be multiple providers involved, face-to-face handoff communications regarding the patients on the service would be critical. Box 8-5, page 159, lists the potential benefits to the bottom line.

Box 8-4. Potential Benefits of a Surgicalist Service

- **More efficient and effective use of OR staff and anesthesia:** This system would minimize utilization of after-hours staff, reduce overtime costs and staff fatigue, and increase satisfaction because surgicalist and late-call surgeons would be able to schedule subacute surgical issues during regular business hours the following day, to be completed by the surgicalist of the day.
- **Enhanced response time for hospital consults and ER needs:**
  - This system would increase satisfaction of the physician base served by the surgicalist team (ER physicians and hospitalist service).
  - The system would potentially improve outcomes for acute surgical conditions due to more rapid response time.
- **Improved OR efficiency:** This system avoids OR delays due to the on-call (elective) surgeon having to evaluate and manage urgent ER/hospital needs between cases or clinic patients.
- **Potential significant contribution to quality improvement:** The surgicalist service could develop protocols to improve care in several arenas, including postoperative pulmonary management. In addition, the surgicalist service could expand multidisciplinary rounds to a broader group of surgical patients.
- **Reduced number of "inappropriate" admission days:**
  - It is not unusual for a patient with a subacute problem (for example, subacute gallbladder) to be admitted and not scheduled for surgery the following day due to the admitting surgeon's schedule. If the surgeon's schedule for the following day is already full, the patient may not get to the OR until the following day. In essence, the patient will have occupied a hospital bed that could have been vacant 24 to 36 hours earlier. Consider this example: On Monday night, the on-call surgeon sees a patient with subacute cholecystitis in the ER. The patient needs surgery but not urgently. The surgeon has a full clinic on Tuesday morning, followed by surgical cases from noon to 8 P.M. The surgeon is concerned about the safety of doing a case postcall after a full day and decides not to do the case "to follow" his or her last elective case. He or she has two options:
    - Do the case on Monday night, using after-hours personnel.

(continued)

157

Box 8-4. Potential Benefits of a Surgicalist Service,
continued

- Schedule the case for Wednesday and discharge the patient Thursday morning.
- **Eliminated call-related clinic cancellations and attendant lost and delayed revenue:**
  - The system would increase patient satisfaction.
  - The system would prevent elective patients from being canceled due to delays related to call.
  - The system would prevent patient loss due to clinic cancellation.
- **Reduced opportunity costs:** This system allows completion of a full OR/clinic schedule for elective surgeons on their call days.
- **Reduced or eliminated costs of unused clinic personnel:** This system prevents canceled clinics, which result in office personnel being underutilized or unutilized. As a result, it enhances clinic personnel satisfaction.

Source: © 2010 Michael S. Woods, M.D., M.M.M.

My back-of-the-napkin math is not unsubstantiated by others' experiences. In 2004 Thomas Memorial Hospital in South Charleston, West Virginia, had two of eight general surgeons quit taking call, and four others simply left the hospital. The two remaining surgeons were, as one would expect, getting crushed. The hospital contracted with two contract surgicalists for $800,000 a year, a seemingly massive outlay of cash. The hospital collected $500,000 on the surgicalists' services, leaving a shortfall of $300,000. This six-figure gap evaporated in the face of soaring surgical revenues from the hiring of another two surgeons, who were guaranteed that the surgicalist services would remain. Thomas Memorial made $1.6 million over and above the cost of the surgicalist program.[16] The model works, but standard accounting evaluation and business-as-usual approaches would have killed this deal.

The upshot of employing a surgicalist model is not just revenue but, more importantly, satisfied providers, staff, and patients.

Box 8-5. Financial Rationale for a Surgicalist Program

- **An acute care surgery service *may* be a loss leader, using direct standard financial measures of productivity.**
- **The greatest financial benefit may be in cost *avoidance* due to:**
  - Improved OR efficiency
  - Reduced use of OR and recovery personnel after hours (This may, directly or indirectly, reduce OR staff turnover and improve retention.)
  - Reduction in "inappropriate" admission days and bed utilization
- **The program has the potential for enhancing surgical revenues.** For example, in one hospital, the average general surgery patient in 2007 was valued at $717.58 (averaging all paying encounters, office visits plus surgery).[17] Therefore, canceling 10 new office patients cost the surgeon/practice about $7,175.83, and canceling 20 new patients cost about $14,351.67. While canceled patients may ultimately generate revenue if rescheduled, that revenue will be delayed. In addition, some patients will not reschedule in the clinic and will be lost from the practice.
- **The revenue the hospital loses when a clinic patient is canceled is significant and could be two to three times the amount the clinic loses.** Total financial loss to an organization with an employed surgeon practice per day of canceled clinic could, depending on how many patients were canceled, easily exceed $20,000 per day.

Source: © 2010 Michael S. Woods, M.D., M.M.M.

List three improvements or modifications to this innovation that you think might improve it:

1. _____

2. _____

3. _____

The Linchpin of the Future

The world of health care is dynamic and untamed, gobbling up nearly 5% of the U.S. economy. Everywhere one looks, there are problems and challenges and issues that we have all colluded in creating. No one is innocent.

The professionals who deliver care to the patient population have, for too long, abdicated responsibility for leading the industry, allowing for-profit insurers, state and federal regulators, and even patients to force change upon us, often with profound unintended negative consequences. HIPAA, EMTALA, declining reimbursement from profit-driven insurers who line their pockets with the dollars meant to pay for care, the AMA's and organized medicine's nearsighted collusion in creating the very access crisis we face today . . . it all adds up to inefficiency, expense, and dissatisfaction. It is no wonder that short tempers flare in the C-suite of our health care organizations and that physicians and nurses act with incivility.

It is time that providers, physicians, nurses, pharmacists, therapists, aides—everyone who is a cog in the wheel of patient care—reclaim their individual professions and the industry as a whole. The first step is to demand civility in the workplace and to stop tolerating—enabling—incivility and the kinds of behavior that result in unhappy, dissatisfied caregivers and the unsafe environment incivility spawns. There is no excuse for individuals being so intimidated or scared by coworkers, whether peers or superiors, that they will not call them to avoid potential errors.

Only dramatic, sweeping change will save the U.S. health care system from itself. Innovation—real innovation—outside the ossified centers of health care will be required in every area of the industry, from insurance, to reimbursement, to training. And especially with regard to relationships. Driving such innovation will require effective, respected communicators . . . individuals who listen and hear, who are driven by civility, and who are trusted by many.

We will, to use an overly dramatic, but true statement, sink or swim together. We are all part of a complex team in a complex industry, taking care of complex problems, in a world that is dynamic, unpredictable, and nonlinear.

As you have learned in this book, communication is the basis of trust. Trust is the basis of patient treatment compliance and respect. And respectful communication is the driver of all relationships. Safe care pivots on effective communication, not just with the patient but between providers. Quality outcomes result from safe care, and the smaller the number of poor outcomes, the more profitable an organization becomes.

Relationship-based civil leadership, based on Drucker's competencies, Bennis's self-reflection, and the Principles of Civility, is part of the basis of Maister's Causal Model for profitability. But more importantly, it is the basis for achieving all that needs to be changed that the provider can directly affect. And this isn't just about physicians. Relationship-based civil leadership is needed from the C-suite all the way through the organization. The principles are easy to teach and model. One doesn't need a manual to interpret what is or is not appropriate in terms of relationship-based civil leadership; anyone in an organization can hold any other individual accountable for his or her behavior at any time. As this begins to happen, interesting things will begin to be realized. Fewer medication errors. Improved quality outcomes. Friendly hallway exchanges, based on authentic civility. In other words, the entire culture of the organization will begin to shift, creating an environment where safety and quality happen.

Providers of health care now have a guide to achieving such relationship-based civility within their organization. They can adopt the standards for medical staff professionalism and behavior contained in Chapter 7, as well as the accountability rules. They don't need to reinvent anything.

There are few things, seemingly, in our professional lives, that are requirements and also enhance our sense of well-being. Relationship-based civil leadership is, however, something that can do just that. The beautiful thing is that by doing the right thing, not only do you personally feel better, you will profit in other ways, including financially. It's time. Just do it. Be civil.

References

1. Levin L.: *Top Teams in Tough Times: 7 Essential Practices.* Atlanta: The Levin Group, 2007.
2. James J: *Thinking in the Future Tense: A Workout for the Mind.* New York: Free Press, 1997.
3. Richman B., et al.: Lessons from India in organizational innovation: A tale of two heart hospitals. *Health Aff (Millwood)* 27:1260–1270, Sep.–Oct. 2008.
4. Christensen C.M.: *The Innovator's Dilemma: When New Technologies Cause Great Firms to Fail.* Cambridge, MA: Harvard Business School Press, 1997.
5. Christensen C.M., Bohmer R., Kenagy J.: Will disruptive innovations cure health care? *Harv Bus Rev* 78:102–117, Sep.–Oct. 2000.
6. Medical bills leading cause of bankruptcy, Harvard study finds. *Consumer Affairs,* Feb. 3, 2005. http://www.consumeraffairs.com/news04/2005/bankruptcy_study.html (accessed Feb. 24, 2010).
7. Cohan P.: Corporate loan default rate spiking. *Blogging Stocks,* Sep. 5, 2008. http://www.bloggingstocks.com/2008/09/05/corporate-loan-default-rate-spiking/ (accessed Feb. 24, 2010).
8. U.S. Department of Education: *Student Loan Default Rates Remain Low.* Sep. 16, 2008. http://www.ed.gov/news/pressreleases/2008/09/09162008a.html (accessed Feb. 24, 2010).
9. Schumacher R.M., Webb J.M., Johnson K.R.: *How to Select an Electronic Health Record System That Healthcare Professionals Can Use.* Feb. 5, 2009. http://www.usercentric.com/publications/2009/02/05/how-select-electronic-health-record-system-healthcare-professionals-can-use (accessed Feb. 6, 2010).
10. Krug S.: *Don't Make Me Think: A Common Sense Approach to Web Usability.* Berkeley, CA: New Riders Press, 2006.
11. Upton D.M., Starts B.R.: Radically simple IT. *Harv Bus Rev,* Mar. 2008. http://hbr.org/2008/03/radically-simple-it/ar/1 (accessed Feb. 6, 2010).
12. Jana R: A shot in the arm for e-health. *BusinessWeek* pp. 58–59, Dec. 8, 2008.
13. The Lewin Group: *Emergency Department Overload: A Growing Crisis—The Results of the American Hospital Association Survey of Emergency Department and Hospital Capacity.* Falls Church, VA: American Hospital Association, 2002.
14. Maa J., et al.: The surgical hospitalist: A new solution for emergency surgical care? *Bull Am Coll Surg* 92:8–17, Nov. 2007.
15. American College of Surgeons: *Statement on Emergency Surgical Care.* http://www.facs.org/fellows_info/statements/st-56.html (accessed Feb. 24, 2010).
16. Horlbeck F.: New breed of surgeons declares, "Have scalpel, will travel." *Triangle Business Journal,* Dec. 1, 2006. http://triangle.bizjournals.com/triangle/stories/2006/12/04/story9.html (accessed Feb. 24, 2010).
17. Woods M.S.: Unpublished data on file.

About the Author

Michael S. Woods, M.D., M.M.M.

Dr. Michael Woods—leadership expert, surgeon, author of *In A Blink, Healing Words,* and *The DEPO Principle,* and editor of *Cultural Sensitivity: A Pocket Guide for Health Care Providers*—is known for his work related to the power of apology and truth-telling in the aftermath of health care errors. Woods is a recognized authority and frequently invited speaker on provider–patient communication and relationships, patient satisfaction, and strategies to reduce medical malpractice.

Dr. Woods is the founder of Civility Mutual Educational Services (http://www.civilitymutual.com), an organization dedicated to helping physicians and health care staff with relationship-based care and improving patient–provider communications and thus raise the bar on health care quality, outcomes, and patient safety. The business plan for Civility Mutual was runner-up at USC's Lloyd Greif Center for Entrepreneurial Studies, which was ranked number one in U.S. graduate business schools for entrepreneurship by *Entrepreneur Magazine* in 2008. Civility Mutual's educational contents have been converted to a set of comprehensive Web-based e-learning courses by PerforMax[3], Inc. (http://www.performax3.com), an e-learning company specializing in customized educational solutions.

Dr. Woods has an active speaking career; his clients have included The Joint Commission, the Department of Defense, the U.S. Army Medical Command, the American Society of Cataract and Refractive Surgery, OhioHealth, Texas Children's Hospital, and the New York Northern Metropolitan Hospital Association. Dr. Woods, a board-certified general surgeon, holds a master's of medical management from the University of Southern California and is a fellow of the American College of Surgeons, a member of the American College of Physician Executives, and a member of the Communications Advisory Panel of the Joint Commission's International Patient Safety Center. Dr. Woods is currently a Chief Medical Officer and a practicing surgeon in a rural New England hospital.

Dr. Woods can be contacted at civilitymutual@me.com.

Index